CITIES OF THE BIBLICAL WORLD

# MEGIDDO

Graham I. Davies

*Lecturer in Divinity*
*University of Cambridge*

## LUTTERWORTH PRESS
CAMBRIDGE

CITIES OF THE BIBLICAL WORLD

General Editor: Graham I. Davies,
Lecturer in Divinity, University of Cambridge

Other Titles:
*Excavation in Palestine*, Roger Moorey, Senior Assistant Keeper,
  Department of Antiquities, Ashmolean Museum, Oxford
*Qumran*, Philip R. Davies, Lecturer in Biblical Studies,
  University of Sheffield
*Jericho*, John R. Bartlett, Lecturer in Divinity and Fellow of
  Trinity College, Dublin
*Ugarit (Ras Shamra)*, Adrian H. W. Curtis, Lecturer in Old
  Testament Studies, University of Manchester

*British Library Cataloguing in Publication Data*

Davies, G. I.
  Megiddo.
  1. Megiddo (Ancient city) 2. Israel—
  Antiquities 3. Excavations (Archaeology—
  Israel—Megiddo, Ancient city
  I. Title
  933      DS110.M4

  ISBN 0–7188–2586–1

First published in 1986 by
**Lutterworth Press**
**7 All Saints' Passage**
**Cambridge CB2 3LS**
Copyright © Graham I. Davies 1986

First American edition published 1986 through special arrangement with Lutterworth by Wm. B. Eerdmans
Publishing Co., 255 Jefferson S.E., Grand Rapids, MI 49503

ISBN 0–8028–0247–8

Photoset and printed in Great Britain by
Redwood Burn Limited, Trowbridge, Wiltshire

# Contents

# Preface

My interest in Megiddo could be said to have begun with some undergraduate essays which I wrote in 1969 under the guidance of Dame Kathleen Kenyon, when she was Principal of St Hugh's College, Oxford. It was a great privilege to be taught by her, and since then I have been fortunate in having my archaeological education extended through the help of a number of friends, especially David Ussishkin and Gabriel Barkay during the excavations at Lachish sponsored by Tel Aviv University. Nevertheless I remain essentially an observer of the archaeological scene and, while this book does contain one or two new suggestions, I have regarded it as my principal aim to draw together the conclusions already reached by others who are better qualified than I am to unravel the complicated history of this fascinating site. Of course the specialists do not always agree, and in a book of this size it is not possible to present every alternative theory to the reader in the detail which it deserves. Perhaps this small book, which is designed with non-specialists in mind, will also encourage a professional archaeologist to undertake the rewarding task of writing a comprehensive account of the site, which I suspect will occupy several large volumes. If so, I hope that my occasional references to the reports on the German excavations at the beginning of this century will serve as a reminder of their great interest and value.

In connection with the writing of this book I wish to express particular thanks to the following for their help: to Lutterworth Press, for their understanding, and patience with the consequent delay, when in the summer of 1982 I decided to change the subject of my contribution to the 'Cities of the Biblical World' series, and for their care and attention during the production of the book (here David Game deserves special mention); to the staff of the West Room of the University Library in Cambridge, for their cheerful assistance at all times; to the Managers of the Bethune-Baker and Hort Memorial Funds of Cambridge University, for grants which made it possible for me to consult the Megiddo archives in Chicago, and to Dr John Larsen, the Museum Archivist at the Oriental Institute, for his willing assistance with my enquiries; to Mr Robert Hamilton, formerly Director of Antiquities in Palestine, for sharing with me his recollections of the American excavations; to the Warden and Fellows of Merton College, Oxford, for electing me into a Visiting Research Fellowship for the Hilary Term, 1985, which enabled me to complete this book in the incomparable surroundings of that College; to Dr Roger Moorey of the Ashmolean Museum and Professor John Emerton of the University of Cambridge, for finding time to read the original manuscript and for many helpful suggestions; to Andrew Brown, whose skilful and intelligent draughtsmanship has produced such excellent drawings to accompany the text; and to Judith Hadley, for her meticulous checking of the proofs.

I am also grateful to Richard Cleave, of Pictorial Archive Inc., of Jerusalem, and Ted Todd, now in Rome, for permission to use photographs from their collections; to the British Academy for permission to reproduce figure 16 from Y. Yadin, *Hazor*, Schweich Lectures for 1971, figure 39; to the Deutscher Palästina-Verein and its President, Professor H. Donner, for permission to reproduce figures 9, 19 and 22 from the published reports on Schumacher's excavations; to A. and C. Black Ltd, for permission to cite a passage from *The Letters of Gertrude Bell*, originally published by Ernest Benn Limited in 1927; to Princeton University Press, for permission to quote extracts from *Ancient Near Eastern Texts Relating to the Old Testament*, ed. J. B. Pritchard, 3rd edition (1969); to the Ordnance Survey, for permission to base figure 12 on one of their maps; and to the Oriental Institute of the University of Chicago, for permission to reproduce numerous photographs and drawings from their publications, to cite extracts from the excavation diary of G. Loud, and to consult and make reference to other unpublished material in their archives.

*Cambridge, February 1986*                                                      G.I. DAVIES

# Abbreviations

| | |
|---|---|
| *AJSL* | *American Journal of Semitic Languages and Literatures*, Chicago. |
| *ANET* | *Ancient Near Eastern Texts Relating to the Old Testament*, ed. J. B. Pritchard, 3rd. ed. (Princeton, 1969). |
| *BA* | *The Biblical Archaeologist*, Philadelphia. |
| *BASOR* | *Bulletin of the American Schools of Oriental Research*, Philadelphia. |
| *IEJ* | *Israel Exploration Journal*, Jerusalem. |
| *OIP* | *Oriental Institute Publications*, Chicago. |
| *PEQ* | *Palestine Exploration Quarterly*, London. |
| *SAOC* | *Studies in Ancient Oriental Civilisation*, Chicago. |
| *ZDPV* | *Zeitschrift der deutschen Palästina-Vereins*, Wiesbaden. |

EB I etc.  Early Bronze Age I etc. ⎫
MB I etc.  Middle Bronze Age I etc. ⎬ (see Chronological Table)
LB I etc.  Late Bronze Age I etc. ⎭

## Notes to the Reader

1. The strata or archaeological layers referred to in this book are those defined by the American excavations (1925–39). The numbering begins with the top (i.e. latest) layer (I) and ends with the lowest (i.e. earliest) layer (XX). The symbol '−XX' refers to remains on and in the bedrock below the lowest complete layer. For fuller details (e.g. of dates) see the Chronological Table on p. viii–ix.

2. The suggestions for further reading at the end of each chapter are primarily

intended for students and others who need to consult the technical literature relating to the site. Those with a more general interest in archaeology could usefully consult:

Y. Aharoni, *The Land of the Bible*, 2nd ed. (Burns and Oates, London, 1979)

K. M. Kenyon, *Royal Cities of the Old Testament* (Barrie and Jenkins, London, 1971)

K. M. Kenyon, *Archaeology in the Holy Land*, 4th ed. (Ernest Benn, London, 1979)

Roger Moorey, *Excavation in Palestine* (Lutterworth Press, Cambridge, 1981)

# Chronological Table

| Archaeological Periods in Palestine | Megiddo Strata | | Wider History |
|---|---|---|---|
| BC | | | BC |
| 8500–4000 Neolithic | | | |
| | Stratum XX (early phase) | | |
| 4000–3100 Chalcolithic | | | |
| (3500–3100 Proto-urban) | Strata XX (later phase)–XIX | | |
| 3100–2700 Early Bronze Age I–II | Stratum XVIII | | 3200–2200 Egyptian Archaic Period and Old Kingdom |
| 2700–2300 Early Bronze Age III | Strata XVII–XVI | | |
| 2300–2000 Early Bronze Age IV (or Middle Bronze I or Intermediate Early Bronze-Middle Bronze Period) | Strata XV–XIV | | 2200–2040 First Intermediate Period in Egypt |
| 2000–1750 Middle Bronze Age I (or Middle Bronze IIA) | Stratum XIII | | 2040–1786 Egyptian Middle Kingdom |
| 1750–1550 Middle Bronze Age II (or Middle Bronze IIB–C) | Strata XII–X | | 1786–1550 Second Intermediate Period in Egypt ('Hyksos') |
| | Stratum IX (AA) | | |
| 1550–1400 Late Bronze Age I | | Strata IX–VIIB (BB) | 1550–1070 Egyptian New Kingdom |
| | | | c. 1468 Invasion of Tuthmosis III |
| 1400–1300 Late Bronze Age IIA | Stratum VIII (AA and DD) | | |
| | Stratum VIIB (AA and DD) | Stratum VIIA (BB) | 1364–1347 Reign of Amenophis IV/Akhenaten (Amarna period) |
| 1300–1200 Late Bronze Age IIB | Stratum VIIA (AA and DD) | | Arrival of Israelites and Philistines in Canaan |

| Archaeological Periods in Palestine | Megiddo Strata | Wider History |
|---|---|---|
| BC | | BC |
| 1200–900   Iron Age I (*or* 1200–1000) | Strata VIB–VIA | |
| | Stratum VB | 1010–970   Reign of David |
| | Stratum VA/IVB | 970–930   Reign of Solomon |
| | | *c*.925   Invasion of Sheshonq I |
| 900–600   Iron Age II | Stratum IVA | 734–3   Invasions of Tiglath-Pileser III of Assyria |
| | Strata III–II | Assyrian rule in Northern Palestine |
| | | 640–609   Reign of Josiah |
| 605–539   Babylonian Period | | |
| 539–332   Persian Period | Stratum I | |
| 332–31   Hellenistic Period | | 332   Alexander the Great in Palestine |
| 31–AD324   Roman Empire | New settlement at Lejjun (Caparcotnae/Legio/ Maximianopolis) | AD66–70   First Jewish Revolt AD132–5   Second Jewish Revolt |

*Note*

The dates for the archaeological periods to the end of Iron Age II are round figures and necessarily approximate. The Megiddo strata are those defined by the American expedition (1925–39): as will be clear from the text of this book, they sometimes include finds of more than one period and the dates attributed to them here are only for general guidance. In some cases they reflect viewpoints adopted in this book with which some scholars would disagree. The dates in the third column are based (where there is disagreement) on the chronological systems referred to at the end of the appropriate chapters of this book.

# List of Illustrations

# 1

# The Identification of Megiddo and its Geographical Setting

Tell el-Mutesellim ('the tell of the governor' in Arabic) is a large mound at the foot of the north-east flank of the Carmel ridge, about 40 km from the point where it juts out into the Mediterranean Sea. It lies on the south-west boundary of the great plain of Esdraelon (or Jezreel), which provides one of the very few easy cross-country routes from the coastal plain of Palestine to the Jordan valley, the sea of Galilee and the countries beyond. Just over a kilometre to the south there emerges into the plain the pass (Wadi Ara) which has been the most popular route across the neck of the Carmel ridge for travellers making these journeys and even, surprisingly at first glance, for many seeking to follow the coast road north. The shoreline around the tip of Carmel is so narrow, and the coast beyond it was once so marshy, that such travellers have at most periods of history chosen instead to cross by Wadi Ara to the plain of Jezreel and then make for Acco (Acre) by a more inland route.

## Identification

This mound (plate 1), it is now known, contains the ruins of Megiddo, one of the great cities of ancient Palestine in the pre-Christian centuries. The modest settlements which are now to be found in this area make it difficult to imagine that there was once a line of great fortified cities along this edge of the plain, whose names are to be found in more than one Biblical passage, as well as in the literature of ancient Egypt, several of whose kings recorded in stone the names of the cities which they conquered in their invasions of their northern neighbour. The book of Joshua, for example, reports that

> In Issachar and Asher Manasseh had Beth-shean and its villages, and Ible-am and its villages, and the inhabitants of Dor and its villages, and the inhabitants of En-dor and its villages, and the inhabitants of Taanach and its villages, and the inhabitants of Megiddo and its villages. (17:11)

The identification of Tell el-Mutesellim as the site of Megiddo was not won without a struggle. For many centuries after it was abandoned *c.* 330 BC the

1

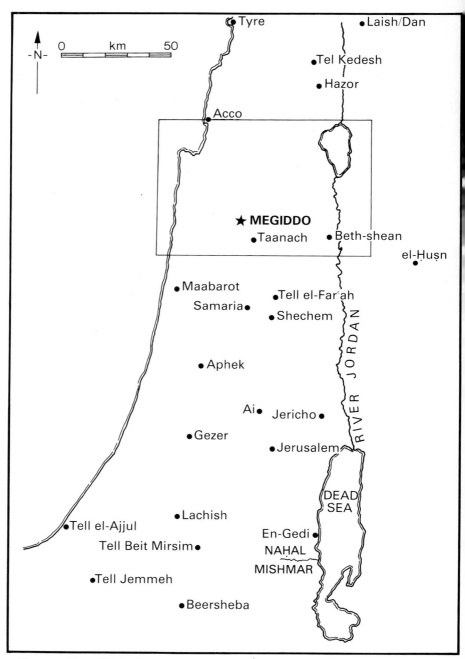

Figure 1 Map of Palestine showing places referred to in the text. (Andrew Brown)

Plate 1   Tell el-Mutesellim from the south (R. L. W. Cleave: Pictorial Archive Inc.,
Jerusalem)

location of Megiddo was forgotten. Jerome in the late fourth century AD had
only a vague idea of where it was. The map of Marino Sanuto (fourteenth century) located it at Sububa, presumably the village known more recently as
Ezbuba, 6 km south-east of the true site. This he may have deduced from the
frequent connection in the Bible between Megiddo and Taanach, the name of
Taanach being clearly preserved in the Arab village of Ti'inik 5 km south of
Ezbuba. The first to come close to the true identification was Esthori
Haparchi, a Jewish writer of the early fourteenth century. A native of France
who subsequently studied in Spain, he emigrated to the Holy Land in 1313
and, after a brief stay in Jerusalem, settled at Beisan (Beth-shean) where he
worked as a doctor. He was also, however, an enthusiastic and intelligent
explorer and in 1322 he completed a book about the Holy Land called *Caphtor
Wapherach*. In it there is the following brief reference to Megiddo: 'Let us
return to Shunem: about two hours directly to the west of it is Megiddo, and it
is (now) called Lejjun. One hour to the south of Megiddo is Taanach – its
name has not changed.' (*Caphtor Wapherach* ed. Luncz, p. 293) Lejjun was an
Arab village located a little over 1 km south of Tell el-Mutesellim (on its own
origin and history see pp. 110–11). As far as we know, nobody had suggested this
identification for Megiddo before, and unfortunately Haparchi does not give

3

his reasons for proposing it. It was subsequently forgotten and was put forward again as a new discovery over five hundred years later by Edward Robinson, the American biblical scholar and explorer, who visited the Holy Land in 1838 and 1852 and greatly advanced the science of biblical geography. (Robinson later discovered that his suggestion had been anticipated by Haparchi and also by two German writers who preceded him by only a few years.) On his first visit to Palestine he did not go to Lejjun, but it was pointed out to him as he crossed the plain some miles to the east. He recognised the Arabic name as a corruption of 'Legio', which had been the name of a well-known Roman city in this area, and he went on to give a series of reasons for locating Megiddo at the same spot, concluding: 'All these circumstances make out a strong case in favour of the identity of Legio and Megiddo; and leave in my own mind little doubt upon the point.' (*Biblical Researches*, 1st ed., vol. 3, p. 180.)

When he returned to Palestine in April 1852 Robinson actually visited not only Lejjun but Tell el-Mutesellim, and saw no reason to change his theory:

> The prospect from the Tell [i.e. Tell el-Mutesellim] is a noble one; embracing the whole of the glorious plain; than which there is not a richer upon earth. . . . A city situated either on the Tell or on the ridge behind it, would naturally give its name to the adjacent plain and waters; as we know was the case with Megiddo and Legio. The Tell would indeed present a splendid site for a city; *but there is no trace, of any kind to show that a city ever stood there.* Legio, as we shall see, was situated on a different spot (my italics). (*Biblical Researches*, 2nd ed., vol. 3, p. 117.)

It seems remarkable now that, after perceiving so clearly the strategic advantages of the tell's location, Robinson failed to identify it as the site of ancient Megiddo. We have to remember that he was quite unaware of the true nature of the tells whose existence he often reported in the course of his *Biblical Researches*. He had no idea that, as Flinders Petrie was to demonstrate so vividly in his excavations at Tell el-Hesi in 1890, each of these tells was a 'mound of many cities', built up over centuries by the superimposition of the ruins and debris of one period of occupation after another. Consequently he only identified the tells with ancient sites when he could discern ruins on them. At Tell el-Mutesellim there were no ruins – though Robinson may have missed some, because (as he tells us) the summit was 'now covered with a fine crop of wheat' – and so he concluded that it could not be an ancient site.

Before general agreement was reached on the precise location of Megiddo, Robinson's apparently successful detective-work was to find a very eminent and persistent critic in Claude Reignier Conder, the British army officer whose name (together with that of H. H. (later Lord) Kitchener) became most closely associated with the Palestine Exploration Fund's Survey of Western

Palestine. The latter bore fruit from 1881 onwards in the publication of the first really accurate map of Western Palestine and of three volumes of *Memoirs* describing the land and its antiquities. In the second volume of these *Memoirs* Conder vigorously rejected the identification of Megiddo with Lejjun, and proposed instead to locate Megiddo at Khirbet Mujedda', a large ruin on the western slopes of the Jordan valley, which he believed had accurately preserved the ancient name and which (according to him) enabled good sense to be made of the various biblical and other references to Megiddo. The pages of the *Quarterly Statement* of the Palestine Exploration Fund resounded with the salvoes of this controversy for a number of years and it was still sufficiently alive in 1892 for the young George Adam Smith to think it necessary to enter the lists against the eminent surveyor in a long footnote in *The Expositor*, the elements of which (in due course appropriately enlarged) were reproduced as an appendix to the chapter on Esdraelon in his famous *Historical Geography of the Holy Land*.

A location for Megiddo in the general vicinity of Lejjun is clearly indicated by the textual evidence, which has been augmented in modern times by discoveries of Egyptian and Canaanite texts. Several biblical passages mention Megiddo in connection with such places as Beth-shean, Taanach and Jezreel, all of which have been securely located by the preservation of the ancient name in an Arabic form (Joshua 17:11, Judges 1:27, 1 Kings 4:12, 2 Kings 9:27, 1 Chronicles 7:29): it follows from this that Megiddo must itself lie somewhere in north central Palestine. The possibilities are narrowed down by the fact that it is a place where Josiah could intercept Pharaoh Neco on his march north to Syria (2 Kings 23:29–30, 2 Chronicles 35:22), by its proximity to Taanach, which is evident both in the Bible (Judges 5:19) and in a Canaanite text of the fifteenth century BC (Taanach Letter 5), and by its choice as a refuge by Ahaziah of Judah as he fled from Jezreel before Jehu's attack from the east (2 Kings 9:27). That it was a little to the north of Taanach is proved by a statement in the annals of Tuthmosis III of Egypt, to the effect that the south wing of the Asiatic army defending Megiddo against him was at Taanach (*ANET*, p. 236). The same annals describe the details of the Pharaoh's approach to Megiddo in such a way as to leave no doubt that it was at or close to Lejjun. The precise identification with Tell el-Mutesellim follows from the archaeological evidence of the excavations, which has made it clear that it was here that a city of the Canaanite and Israelite periods was located, whereas at Lejjun only remains from the Roman period and later have been identified. We can therefore confidently say, despite the fact that the ancient name did not survive in this case and the absence to this day of any inscription from the site which mentions its name, that Tell el-Mutesellim is the site of ancient Megiddo.

## Geographical Setting

The size of the mound was considerably underestimated by early visitors. The PEF Survey described it as 'a long flat-topped mound about 200 yards by 100 (or four acres)'. The true maximum dimensions of the summit, as given by Gottlieb Schumacher's topographical survey of 1903, are about 315 metres from east to west and 230 metres from north to south, and the surface area is upwards of twelve acres. The shape is somewhat irregular, like a pear, with

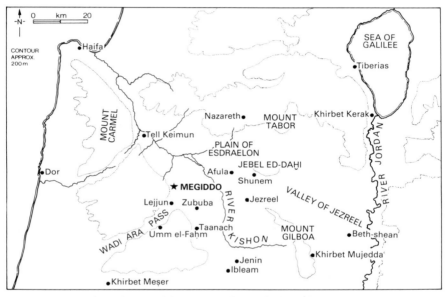

Figure 2 Map of Megiddo and its surroundings. (Andrew Brown)

the narrow end to the west. Before excavation began, the highest point of the mound, in the south-east corner, was about 175 metres above sea level, but in the north, where the main city gates proved to be, there was a hollow, whose lowest point was only about 155 metres above sea level. Below it, and providing a convenient access to the summit, was a flat terrace with some ancient remains, at an average of a little over 140 metres above sea level. Today a site museum and reception area for visitors is located there in buildings erected in the 1930s as the camp of the Chicago expedition.

The mound is situated near the northern end of a low ridge about 1.5 km long which is divided from the hills to the west by a shallow valley (called es-Suq el-Mindessi according to Schumacher's map) and bounded on the south by Wadi el-Lejjun. To the east the ground falls away to the Jezreel plain, which in this region lies about 120 metres above sea level. There is an abundant spring, Ain el-Kubbi, below the northern slopes of the terrace referred to above, but Schumacher commented on the swampy surroundings and the tendency of those who drank its water to contract fever, which deterred even the Bedouin from using it, and better water was to be found a little further away to the north-west at Ain er-Ruzz. Another spring used in antiquity was located in a cave on the south-west slopes of the mound proper.

Large cities (large whether by ancient standards or modern) do not grow up everywhere, but only where the surrounding territory is capable (or can be made capable) of supporting a large population and where particular factors, geographical or political, demand the presence of such centres. It is therefore possible to explain in large measure why cities developed at particular places at different epochs of history by making use of, on the one hand, scientific knowledge about the geology, geography and climate of an area and, on the other, historical information (both from texts and from archaeological excavations) about political conditions, wars, trade and so on. The nexus between settlement patterns and such factors also makes it possible to fill some of the many gaps in our historical evidence by inferring what must have been the case for city life to have been possible.

We have already noticed that Tell el-Mutesellim lies on the boundary of two geographical sub-regions of Palestine, the alluvial plain of Esdraelon (Jezreel) and the hills of the Carmel Ridge. The former (plate 2) is an almost triangular area which is bounded by the Carmel ridge on the south-west, the Nazareth hills on the north, and Mount Tabor, Jebel ed-Dahi ('Little Hermon' or the hill of Moreh) and Mount Gilboa on the east. It slopes very gently to the west (the drop is only about 25 metres in 25 km from south-east to north-west) and is drained by the various tributaries of the river Kishon (Nahr el-Muqatta'), into which a substantial quantity of water also runs off the surrounding hills. The river is one of the few perennial streams of Palestine, but it is no more than twenty feet across even at the point where it leaves Esdraelon near Tell el-Qassis. The problems of drainage caused by the flatness of the plain and its enclosed nature are accentuated in the eastern part by low ridges of basalt (marked today by the houses of the Israeli settlement of Hayogev) which cut into the plain from both sides north of Megiddo. The poor natural drainage used to make for difficult travel in winter and there are several reports from quite modern times of the problems faced by travellers, not to speak (for the present) of the embarrassment caused to Sisera's army according to the fifth

Plate 2  The plain of Esdraelon seen from the summit of Tell el-Mutesellim (G. I. Davies)

chapter of the book of Judges. For example, the generally courageous traveller Gertrude Bell wrote of a journey from Haifa to Jenin in February 1905:

> Moreover the road lay all across the Plain of Esdraelon (which is without doubt the widest plain in the world) and the mud was incredible. We waded sometimes for an hour at a time knee deep in clinging mud, the mules fell down, the donkeys almost disappeared ('By God!', said one of the muleteers, 'you could see nothing but his ears') and the horses grew wearier and wearier. (*Letters*, vol. 1, p. 176.)

This probably helps to account for the fact that in ancient times there were very few settlements in the central part of the plain near the Kishon: the emptiness of the area between Megiddo, Afula, Jezreel and Jenin is particularly striking. Coupled with the problem of drainage is the incidence of malaria, which troubled the German excavators at Megiddo in 1903–5 and the Americans in the 1920s.

It would, however, be a mistake to exaggerate the consequences of these difficulties for the agricultural exploitation of the plain, and even for travel within it, in ancient times. Genesis 49:15 speaks of the 'pleasantness' of the land of Issachar, the tribal territory which most nearly corresponds to the plain. The difficulties for travellers are largely seasonal, being severe only in the winter months, and the basalt ridges north of Megiddo referred to earlier provided an easier passage across the breadth of the plain which may well have been the regular road in that area in antiquity (rather than the present more easterly route to Afula). It could well be that in this as in other parts of the ancient world drainage schemes served to mitigate the consequences of the natural lie of the land. Certainly it is incorrect to suppose that the plain was uncultivable except in small areas until the 1920s, for the officers of the PEF Survey reported that in 1872 the great majority of the plain was under cultivation, the problem in recent times having been not the poor drainage but raiders and Bedouin encampments. Given the right political conditions it seems likely that large areas could have been under cultivation in antiquity. The absence of settlements is no objection, for cultivation could have been organised from the large cities on the edge of the plain, like Megiddo. One of the Amarna letters from Megiddo (see below, pp. 59–60) speaks of the ruler of Megiddo organising agricultural labourers even at Shunem, on the far side of the plain. Of the richness of the plain when it is cultivated there is no doubt, given the fertile alluvial soil and the ample rainfall. In the nineteenth century AD the main products were wheat, barley and millet, with a little sesame, castor-oil and cotton.

The hilly hinterland of Megiddo is of a different character north and south of Wadi Ara, because of the geology of the area. The hills to the south, known in modern times as the Sheikh Iskander hills or the Heights (Ramoth) of Manasseh, are of the same Cenomanian limestone as Mount Carmel itself and the bulk of the central hill country of Palestine. This is the type of stone preferred for building and it breaks down to form a fertile deep-red soil known as *terra rossa*. The natural vegetation is evergreen forest and scrub, which together with the broken lie of the land constitutes a formidable obstacle to progress. Where the forest is cleared, however, the land is productive and could have supported crops such as vines and olives, as it has done in modern times. Many presses for wine or oil are cut into the rock in this area, and others were found in the excavations at Taanach and Megiddo. There is evidence of sporadic settlement here in some periods of antiquity. Iron ore is found near Umm el-Fahm. The more northerly hills are lower and composed of the Lower Eocene limestone, which has the same chalky character as is found in the Judaean Shephelah. This produces a fine, greyish soil (rendzina), which is less fertile than the *terra rossa* but easier to cultivate with primitive implements and consequently attractive to ancient farmers. The natural vegetation is less dense than in the hills farther south. The area is blessed with high rainfall and many springs, though water supply is a problem in the summer. Ancient settlements were mainly in the western part of this region away from the plain of Jezreel. The hills above Megiddo may perhaps have served for grazing. Because of the characteristics which this region shares with

9

the Judaean Shephelah, some scholars have suggested that it is referred to as 'the Shephelah (low hills) of Israel' in Joshua 11:16 (compare v.2).

Wadi Ara itself, which separates these two areas of higher ground, is one of two valleys (the other emerges into the plain 12 km to the north by Tell Keimun (Jokneam)) which were created when the soft Senonian chalk was exposed at the edge of the syncline, or downfold, which forms the central part of the Carmel ridge above Megiddo. In many parts of Palestine such valleys form important lines of communication, and we have already seen that this is the case here: the chalk has eroded into a relatively easy and straight route through the hills. Nevertheless it was not without its dangers, and an Egyptian scribe of the thirteenth-century BC wrote of the fear which a journey through it could engender:

> The narrow valley is dangerous with Bedouin, hidden under the bushes. Some of them are of four or five cubits . . . and fierce of face. Their hearts are not mild, and they do not listen to wheedling. . . . Thy path is filled with boulders and pebbles, without a *toe hold* for passing by, overgrown with reeds, thorns, *brambles* and 'wolf's paw'. The ravine is on one side of thee, and the mountain rises on the other. (*ANET*, pp. 477–8. See also below, p. 52.)

The city of Megiddo therefore stood in a position where it was possible to exploit rich natural resources of several different kinds but also, as indicated at the beginning, near an important cross-country route. It lay in fact at a junction of several routes: the route along the edge of the plain of Esdraelon from Haifa, Acco and Phoenicia to Beth-shean and the Jordan; the route from the coastal plain across the Carmel ridge via Wadi Ara; and a safe route north across the plain to Galilee and Syria. As a consequence it was easily accessible to traders and migrants from all directions; but at the same time it could, if powerful enough, control access by means of these routes and so direct the course of both trade and war. It is not surprising therefore that it was at most periods of antiquity one of the wealthiest cities of Palestine, or that it was a prize often fought over and when secured strongly defended. Even so, in the great battles in its vicinity of which we know, it several times failed to be an effective barrier against armies invading from the south. Tuthmosis III, Neco and Allenby all managed to defeat those who held the north end of the Wadi Ara pass by superior numbers and generalship. Perhaps after all it was rather trade which ensured that through the centuries there was usually a major centre here. Even down to modern times the khan at Lejjun continued to be a staging-point on the road from Syria to Egypt, and Schumacher reported that during his excavations great herds of camels from Syria would pass the foot of the tell each year in July and August before drinking and resting at the stream in Wadi el-Lejjun, on their way to the Egyptian camel-markets.

*Further reading*

For information about the geography of the region C. R. Conder and H. H. Kitchener, *The Survey of Western Palestine, Memoirs* ..., edited with additions by E. H. Palmer and W. Besant, vol. 2 (London, 1882), pp. 36–50, 73–4, and G. Adam Smith, *Historical Geography of the Holy Land*, 25th ed. (London, 1931), ch. 19, remain invaluable. Among more recent works see D. Baly, *Geography of Palestine*, rev. ed. (Guildford and London, 1974), ch. 13; T. L. Thompson, *The Settlement of Palestine in the Bronze Age* (Wiesbaden, 1979), esp. pp. 33–45; M. Zohary, *Plants of the Bible* (Cambridge, 1982). The identification of Megiddo is treated by E. Robinson, *Biblical Researches in Palestine* (London, 1841), vol. 3, pp. 177–80, and *ibid.*, 2nd ed. (London, 1856), vol. 3, pp. 115–19; Conder and Kitchener, *Survey*, vol. 2, pp. 64–6, 70, 90–9; and Smith, *Historical Geography*, pp. 385–7, 411–12. H. H. Nelson, *The Battle of Megiddo* (Chicago, 1913), was the first thorough topographical study of the relevant part of the annals of Tuthmosis III, and is still useful (but see the corrections of R. O. Faulkner, *Journal of Egyptian Archaeology* 28 (1942), 2–15; L. Christophe, *Revue d'Égyptologie* 6 (1950), 89–114, is ingenious but not ultimately convincing).

The heights above sea-level given by Schumacher are uniformly about 18 metres too high, as comparison with the American measurements shows, and I have corrected them accordingly.

# 2

# The Excavations at
# Tell el-Mutesellim (Megiddo)

It is not surprising to find that a tell of the size and importance described in the previous chapter was one of the earliest to attract the excavator's spade and one of those where a succession of archaeologists have tried to add further precision to our knowledge about its history. As will appear later in this book, the task is by no means completed and there are still some deep-seated problems of interpretation which are unlikely to be solved without yet further excavation. Up to the present the tell has been excavated by a German expedition under the direction of Gottlieb Schumacher between April 1903 and November 1905; by an American expedition from the Oriental Institute at the University of Chicago, directed in turn by Clarence S. Fisher (1925–7), P. L. O. Guy (1927–34), R. S. Lamon (1934–5) and Gordon Loud (1935–9); and by Israeli teams from the Hebrew University of Jerusalem under Yigael Yadin (1960, 1966–7, 1971–2), I. Dunayevsky (1965) and A. Eitan (1974).

## The German Excavations (1903–5)

The German Society for the Study of Palestine (Deutsche Verein zur Erforschung Palästinas, or Deutsche Palästina-Verein (DPV)) was founded in 1877 and had by 1900 established its reputation by sponsoring numerous studies of Palestine, including Hermann Guthe's excavations in Jerusalem and Schumacher's attempt (unfortunately never completed) to complement the Palestine Exploration Fund's Survey of Western Palestine with a similar survey of Transjordan. But it had not so far undertaken the excavation of a tell, such as those which had occupied the Palestine Exploration Fund during the 1890s, and there seems to have been a sense among the Committee of the Society that it was falling behind in the quest for new knowledge. Perhaps a greater spur to activity, because nearer to home, was the fact that in 1902 Professor Ernst Sellin of the University of Vienna had independently begun excavation at the site of ancient Taanach. But broader intellectual currents added their force to the growing sense that a beginning must be made, for discoveries in Egypt and Mesopotamia had already begun to open up new vistas in the history and religion of the ancient Near East. In Germany particularly the 'Babel-Bibel' controversy had been sparked off by the suggestion that a large part of the Old Testament had been borrowed from Egyptian or Babylonian sources, and both sides were anxious for further light on this question from excavations conducted in Palestine itself.

It appears that this latter consideration influenced the choice of a site for excavation, since the cities on the edge of the plain of Esdraelon were known from written sources (such as the Amarna letters) to have been important centres already in Canaanite times. Since Taanach was already 'reserved', Tell el-Mutesellim (Megiddo) was an obvious choice, the more so as it was readily accessible from Haifa, which as well as being a port was one of the major cities of the country. A large part of the cost was defrayed by the Kaiser himself, who had already shown his interest in the Society and in Palestine generally in a number of ways. As director of the excavations Schumacher was an obvious choice since, in addition to experience of excavation which he had gained while working with Sellin at Taanach, he was a trained surveyor. He had also lived in Palestine for many years and was therefore excellently placed to deal with the local people in whatever ways were needed. As was customary at the time, the expedition had a very small core staff but employed large numbers of villagers, men, women and children, under the direction of local foremen, for the digging and the removal of the debris. Dr I. Benzinger (who had published a volume on *Hebräische Archäologie* in 1894) acted as Deputy Director in the autumn of 1903 when Schumacher was absent from the site, and the reports refer to occasional periods spent there by distinguished visitors such as the Hebraist Professor E. Kautzsch.

The work itself began with the drawing of accurate survey maps of the tell (at a scale of 1:1000) and of its wider surroundings, including Lejjun (at 1:5000). The first area to be excavated was the highest point of the tell, which lay near its eastern edge, and here Schumacher identified what he thought were two successive building stages of a 'Temple-fortress' (*Tempelburg*). In the south a fortified gate was uncovered, and Schumacher then began the excavation, from the northern edge of the tell, of a trench twenty metres broad running due south across the summit. This work continued through the autumn of 1903, when caves in the vicinity of the tell were also explored for ancient remains, and on into the excavation seasons of 1904. By broadening his main trench to thirty metres Schumacher was able to expose two buildings which he called the North Fortress (*Nordburg*) and the Central Fortress (*Mittelburg*). The exploration of the summit was extended by the excavation of shallow test-trenches in different directions and attention was also given, by the excavation of further trenches, to the fortifications on the slopes. These Schumacher seems to have regarded as a single system of defence constructed

13

at one and the same time. The Roman theatre and some ruins at Lejjun were also cleared in 1904.

By the following year it was clear that the Turkish authorities, who had granted a permit for the excavations to take place, would not allow them to continue beyond the autumn of 1905 and so, instead of having a pause in the hot summer months (when labour was difficult to come by anyway owing to the harvest), as had been done in the first two years, it was decided to excavate as far as possible all through the summer, in the hope of bringing the work to a satisfactory conclusion. Urgent calls for additional funds were made to the Society's subscribers in order to finance the extra weeks of work. The achievements were considerable, as the two 'fortresses' were extensively investigated and beneath the Central Fortress a series of large subterranean vaulted chambers were found, evidently tombs, some of them still containing skeletons and grave-goods. In a small area in the North Fortress the excavation was continued to the virgin rock, the only place on the tell where bedrock was reached by Schumacher, and deposits that were clearly of great antiquity were found. In addition a very finely constructed corner of walling which jutted into the north-south trench near its southern end became the starting-point for an investigation which brought to light a large enclosed courtyard with what Schumacher called a 'Palace' on its northern side. (It later emerged during the American excavations that this 'Palace' was only a gatehouse to the courtyard, and the real palace lay some distance to the south in an area not touched by Schumacher's work.) Further work was also done on the caves around the tell and other constructions in the vicinity: to the east a group of milestones was found which confirmed that the Roman road to Ptolemais, present-day Acco, had passed close by the tell.

In the report on his work, which was published in 1908, Schumacher attempted to put the various structures which he had found into chronological order. He did not attempt to correlate them precisely with particular periods of history or dates in years BC or AD – this was left for consideration in a second volume – but he sought to establish a relative chronology of his finds, and the report is set out in accordance with his conclusions. He distinguished eight strata, calling the earliest 'I' and the latest 'VIII' (the opposite procedure to that normally used today). He had intended to describe nothing but the buildings in his first volume, and he kept to this plan for his treatment of the two earliest strata. But he found it impossible to maintain a total separation between the buildings and the objects found in them and the later chapters of the report include details of many objects of pottery, stone, metal and other materials. This was extremely fortunate for subsequent research, as almost all Schumacher's unpublished notes and drawings were unaccountably lost before work on the second volume could begin. Without the photographs and descriptions which he included in the later chapters of *Tell el-Mutesellim I* the task of relating his findings to their historical setting, which was bound to be difficult in any case, could never have been attempted.

This task was not attempted until the 1920s and it was then not Schumacher who took it up but Carl Watzinger, a Professor at the University of Tübingen who had had no direct connection with the excavations at Megiddo, but had taken part in other archaeological field-work in Palestine: he had, for example, excavated with Sellin at Jericho. As we have seen, he had practically no information about Schumacher's excavations apart from what the latter had already published. On the other hand the delay did give him some advantages, for in the meantime a number of other sites in Palestine had been excavated and the results published, so that he was able to draw far more comparisons with findings from elsewhere and as a result to arrive at a much more precise chronology than would have been possible at an earlier date. Watzinger's analysis, *Tell el-Mutesellim II*, is a masterpiece of archaeological scholarship for its time and an indispensable companion to the original report. As an experienced archaeologist himself he was able to use Schumacher's often very precise information to correct errors in the latter's grander reconstructions, and his sharp eye perceived from the photographs which had been published that Schumacher's workmen had often continued digging below the floors of buildings, so that finds from a deeper and therefore earlier level were mixed in with those which were in use when a building was destroyed or abandoned. Although these 'intrusive' objects could not be identified conclusively from the limited information about find-spots given in the report, the likelihood that such were present allowed Watzinger to discount objects which would otherwise have required much too long a period of occupation for a particular building.

The first structures which Watzinger discussed were the earliest parts of the North and Central Fortresses (including two underground burial-chambers), which he dated from their architecture and finds to the end of what is now known as the Middle Bronze Age, *c.*1600 BC. The later stages of the 'fortresses' (Watzinger was sceptical about this designation, as they appeared to have little defensive strength) he assigned to the Late Bronze Age, believing that the Central Fortress was destroyed *c.*1400 BC, while the North Fortress, which included some Mycenaean sherds, lasted for approximately a century longer. Little remained in his view of the Megiddo of the next three centuries, at least in the areas excavated. But there were signs of an eventual rebuilding of the city in fine ashlar masonry and since this masonry was thought to be characteristic at other sites of Solomon's time, Watzinger concluded that this stratum (IV) was from the tenth century. The revival was short-lived and a great 'burnt layer' (*Brandschicht*) lay over the ruins of this phase: Watzinger attributed its destruction to the Egyptian king Sheshonq I (945–924), whose campaign in Palestine is commemorated in one of his own inscriptions, in which Megiddo is named (*ANET*, pp. 242–3; see also p. 96 below), and dated by 1 Kings 14:25–6 to the fifth year of Rehoboam, Solomon's son and successor. The 'Palace' found by Schumacher belonged to the next stratum (V) and represented, he thought, a ninth-century reconstruction of the city, along with some smaller structures, all of which were destroyed by the Assyrians in 733 BC. In the *Tempelburg* Watzinger retained the distinction into two phases, but denied that either of them had any religious significance: he attributed the earlier of them, which he thought was a house or part of a residential complex, to the end of Stratum V and the later phase, with its thick walls, he took to be the fortress of the Assyrian governor in Megiddo, whose existence was proved by a cuneiform contract from Assur. In several areas there were modest buildings from the period of Persian rule (sixth to fourth centuries BC), but the only structures on the tell from a later period than this were a medieval Arab watch-tower above the *Tempelburg* and two water-tanks apparently of the same date.

The later excavations at Megiddo (and elsewhere) have shown that Watzinger made a serious mistake in ascribing the construction of the Stratum IV buildings to Solomon and their destruction to Sheshonq I. Both belong at least a century earlier. The reliance on what was thought to be distinctively 'Solomonic' masonry led him astray, even against the evidence of some of the pottery associated with the destruction which he knew was from the beginning of the Iron Age. The quest for Solomonic features at Megiddo, be they masonry, stables or gates, has however been a long and tortuous one and Watzinger was only the first to embark upon it. It should also be noted that the long 'gap' in occupation between *c*.1300 and 900 BC which he observed is, with regard to the earlier part of that period, a substantially correct representation of the remains in the area about which he had the most information, namely that of the two 'fortresses'. Subsequent excavation has shown that in this part of the tell the remains from the Late Bronze Age were largely removed when the site was being prepared for reconstruction in the tenth or the ninth century. Consequently one would naturally gain the impression from excavation in this area alone that the site was unoccupied for a long period in the Late Bronze and early Iron Ages, although it is now clear that there was almost continuous occupation at the site throughout this time.

By 1929, when Watzinger's volume was published, a new expedition to Megiddo had taken the field, but the first adequate account of this work only appeared a few months before *Tell el-Mutesellim II* and Watzinger made very little reference to the new excavations. There is discernible in Professor Albrecht Alt's foreword to his volume a slight sense of grievance that the

16

Americans had gone ahead with the excavation without seeking the agreement of the German Society: it is regarded as 'bad form' to conduct excavations on a site without first checking whether archaeologists who have dug there before intend to return for further work.

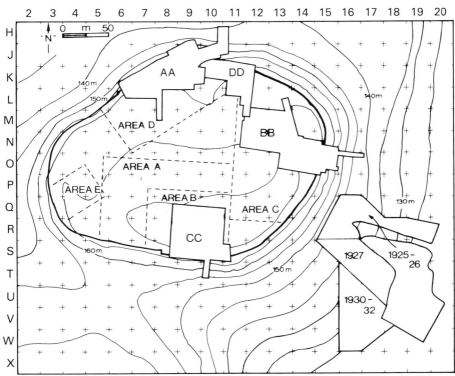

Figure 3  Plan of American excavation areas. The dates at bottom right indicate the parts of the cemetery which were cleared in different seasons. (Andrew Brown; based on G. Loud, *Megiddo II*, figure 377, and P. L. O. Guy and R. M. Engberg, *Megiddo Tombs*, figure 2)

## The American excavations (1925–39) (fig. 3)

The Chicago expedition was the brainchild of the famous Egyptologist James Henry Breasted who, as Director of the Oriental Institute, secured the backing of Mr John D. Rockefeller, Jr, for this part of the Institute's 'grand plan' to advance historical study of the culture of the ancient Near East by excavations at carefully chosen sites in Egypt, Mesopotamia, Asia Minor and the

17

intervening lands. Dr Clarence Fisher, who had shared in the direction of excavations at Samaria before the First World War and at Beth-shean in 1921–3, was appointed Field Director for an operation that was initially envisaged to last for five years. He was in fact to retain this role for less than two years, becoming a victim of the outbreaks of malaria which were unpleasantly frequent in the first seasons of this excavation.

Fisher was an unashamed advocate of the clearance of large areas of a mound layer-by-layer and he clearly regarded Schumacher's 'great trench' as more of a hindrance than a help:

> In the previous section we have seen how the hill was built up layer by layer. It should be obvious that the logical method of determining the extent of the respective remains of each separate town level and securing as complete a record as possible of its character, is to reverse the process and strip off layer after layer, beginning with the topmost or latest in date. (*The Excavation of Armageddon*, p. 26)

Because Fisher and his successors have sometimes been accused of having a very naive idea of the nature of these layers or strata, the following statement of principle should be noted:

> The task is complicated by the fact that, instead of being nicely and evenly differentiated like the layers of a cake, the strata are rarely horizontal throughout and never parallel . . . Successive towns expanded over the edges, either following the natural slopes or built on artificial terraces. (*The Excavation of Armageddon*, p. 27)

Ideally according to this view the whole of a particular stratum should be removed before the next is disturbed, but Fisher believed that this was impracticable in the case of a mound the size of Megiddo and his original intention was to excavate only the portion of the mound east of Schumacher's main trench, where (he supposed) the major buildings of the ancient city lay. Before this could be done, however, he had to organise the building of an excavation headquarters (part of which now comprises the museum beside the tell) and, more significant from an archaeological point of view, to make a fresh survey of the tell and a special examination of the area below its south-eastern slopes, where it was intended to deposit the debris that would be excavated on the summit. This area proved to have been used as a cemetery between the third millennium BC and the Roman period, and by the end of 1926 sixty tombs had been excavated, many of them intact and with impressive collections of grave-goods. Early reports spoke of the discovery of a Neolithic tomb, but this seems to have been due to a misunderstanding of some stone implements, which were later realised to be of no earlier than Bronze Age date.

On the summit Fisher's work was confined to the south-eastern portion of the tell (subsequently known as Area C – see fig. 3), where he investigated further what Schumacher had described as the 'Temple-fortress'. His conclusion (apparently reached independently of Watzinger) was that the two building stages were quite separate, the later being a fortress and the earlier a temple, dedicated to the goddess Astarte. In this interpretation he relied on his own discovery of a number of limestone altars and other objects of an apparently religious nature in an area a little to the south of the 'temple'. As the excavation progressed under the direction of Fisher's successors it became clear that these objects were of a much earlier date and could shed no light on the function of the 'temple' or of the very finely constructed building (later numbered 'Building 338') which Fisher began to uncover underneath it. Unfortunately this was not clear to H. G. May, who perpetuated the myth of the 'Astarte temple' in a supplementary volume to the excavation reports, in which the objects referred to were published. Fisher also identified a number of other buildings and streets, mainly from the latest periods of the city's history.

Guy, who replaced Fisher as Director in the spring of 1927, began by clearing a further area to the south-east of the mound for dumping debris, and discovered another forty-one tombs, as well as a lower circuit of walls which he tentatively dated to the period of David and Solomon. This done he resumed the excavation of the summit and concentrated his efforts in an area north of where Fisher had worked, though still to the east of Schumacher's deep trench. By the end of 1928 he had completed the clearance of the fine building (338) beneath the so-called 'temple' and also exposed, in his new area, parts of a city wall and a complex of what he believed to be the royal stables of Solomon. At the same time larger schemes were in his mind and he was able to persuade Professor Breasted and the Mandatory authorities in Palestine, with further financial help from John D. Rockefeller, Jr, to arrange the compulsory purchase of the whole mound for the Government of Palestine. The aim was to extend the excavation west of Schumacher's trench and so bring to execution Fisher's vision of a whole mound being excavated stratum by stratum to the bottom.

During 1929 the surface debris was cleared from the remainder of the mound, exposing the uppermost layer of ruins (which did not date from the same period in all areas). In the north (Area D) a city gate was excavated, linked to what appeared to be the same solid city wall that had been found in the eastern area: it too was at this stage ascribed to Solomon. Work continued intermittently in this area in the following seasons, but the major efforts of the excavators were increasingly concentrated in Areas A–B and E in the south of the tell (exclusively so from the spring of 1933), where they were rewarded by the discovery in succession of a concealed passage through the city wall leading to a spring, a rock-cut shaft and tunnel giving even more secure access to the same spring, a further set of 'Solomonic stables' and the foundations of the palace whose courtyard and gatehouse Schumacher had earlier found. Between 1931 and 1933 further work was done on the eastern slopes, adding more tombs to the inventory and also some domestic occupation levels from the very earliest periods of the tell's history. By the summer of 1934 the work in the south had reached Stratum VII, a transitional level bridging the end of the Late Bronze Age and the beginning of the Iron Age. At this point Guy resigned from the Directorship: a year later he became Director of the British School of Archaeology in Jerusalem, in succession to J. W. Crowfoot, the excavator of Samaria. It seems likely that, for all his successes, Guy's progress was too slow for his masters at the Oriental Institute and they may have been anxious to relieve him of the Directorship. He deserves, nevertheless, to be remembered for two technical innovations which he pioneered at Megiddo: the use of 'locus numbers' to designate rooms or other small areas in a stratum, which is now a universal practice, and the taking of aerial photographs of major structures by means of a camera attached to a captive balloon.

For over a year, until October 1935, digging on the tell was at a standstill, but the assistant staff used the opportunity to prepare final reports on work done during the previous ten years. The major volumes did not appear until 1938 and 1939, but three specialised studies were published during the interval. As the new Director the Oriental Institute appointed Gordon Loud, who had had recent field experience in the direction of the Institute's excavation at the Assyrian site of Khorsabad (Dur Sharrukin). It would be possible to give a much more precise account of the years of his Directorship, since his excavation diary, preserved in the archives of the Oriental Institute Museum in Chicago, records how work progressed in each area from day to day as well as the interpretation that was put on the finds at the time. This diary thus constitutes an invaluable supplement to the abbreviated account of these years in the text of *Megiddo II*. But in keeping with the character of the remainder of this chapter only the broad outlines of Loud's work will be sketched here. His strategy differed from Guy's both in aim and in technique. He abandoned as impractical the plan of excavating the whole mound, aiming instead to reach bedrock in at least a restricted area (an aim that was only to be fulfilled in the third season of his Directorship). In order to identify the areas where digging would be most productive he laid out three long, narrow test-trenches in the north, north-east and south of the mound. The first two of these cut through respectively a palace and a temple of the Late Bronze Age and became the starting-points for extensive areas of work which were designated as Areas AA and BB to distinguish them from the quite separate areas referred to as A and B in the earlier years of the expedition's work. The third trench (CC), which exposed an early city wall but otherwise only domestic buildings, was abandoned after Loud's first season.

In both the remaining areas evidence of the city's fortifications was found, from the Early Bronze Age onwards in Area BB. Area AA proved to contain a succession of city gates of the Middle Bronze, Late Bronze and Iron Ages, some directly underneath, others a little to the west of, the gate discovered by Guy and attributed to Solomon. Owing to the appearance of a much more massive Iron Age structure immediately below this gate, the latter was now assigned to the later Israelite monarchy and the earlier gate was ascribed to Solomon. The palace which had been touched in the original test-trench proved to have a long history and in rooms of two of its phases collections of ivories and other precious objects were found which gave a vivid demonstration of the wealth and international contacts of Late Bronze Age (Canaanite) Megiddo. In Area BB the temple which was the first to come to light was rich in finds of a cultic character and in later seasons three much earlier phases of sacred architecture were traced, beginning in Stratum XIX, of the Chalcolithic period. This superposition of temples indicated that the area had retained its sanctity over a very long period, probably even when there was no building standing there. To the east and west of the 'temple area' were mainly private houses, though larger (perhaps public) buildings appear from time to time and at one point Loud was able to relate them directly to the 'North Fortress' found by Schumacher. In 1938–9 an additional area, DD, was opened up to try to make a physical connection between the excavations in Areas AA and BB and so correlate the structures in the two areas with each other more definitely than had so far been possible. The excavations reached a further palatial building of the Late Bronze Age (Stratum VIII), but the outbreak of war brought a premature end to the work before the intended final season could establish any link between the two areas.

The report on the first ten years of excavation (*Megiddo I*) was finally published just after the digging finished, in July 1939, the *Tombs* volume having appeared in the preceding year. The report on the remaining seasons was ready for the printer in 1942, though it was not actually published until 1948. The outbreak of the Second World War and especially a shortage of paper placed limits on the extent of this publication, and this must be taken into account when its adequacy is assessed. It lacks the detailed description of the process of excavation and the considered interpretation of the whole site which would ideally be expected in such a report, and Loud's own reference to the work as little more than 'a catalogue of the architecture and artefacts recovered' only anticipates the description that has seemed appropriate to others. Nor is it in every respect a complete catalogue, and several important pieces of unpublished pottery have from time to time been identified by researchers working in the storerooms of the Oriental Institute. There are also gaps in our knowledge which derive not so much from the curtailment of the

21

publication as from the methods of recording (and indeed of excavating) that were employed on the site. Kathleen Kenyon and others pointed out that the 'strata' into which the mound was analysed were sometimes crudely defined, so that tombs on the summit, for example, were associated with the debris layers in which they were constructed rather than with the higher and later living surfaces from which they were excavated by the ancient inhabitants of the site. As a consequence the pottery attributed to a particular stratum is often a mixture of what genuinely derives from that level and period with later pottery found in tombs that were dug into it a century and more afterwards. Great care needs to be exercised in using the lists of pottery types and note must be taken of whether a particular piece was found in a tomb or in a deposit that is directly associated with a building or occupation level.

Nevertheless the achievements of the Megiddo staff should not be under-estimated, and they have enabled other scholars to circumvent to some extent the weaknesses which have been mentioned. The publication of a complete set of plans, stratum by stratum, area by area, with heights of walls and floors marked on them, is a substantial advance on *Megiddo I*, and the preservation of Loud's excavation diary in the archives of the Oriental Institute, together with the photographic records there, provides the possibility of compiling a much more complete account of what was found on the tell – some use of this diary will be made at a later point in this book. As for the objects, a study of the pottery sequence was published by G. M. Shipton in 1939 and it contains many comparisons with the pottery of other sites. The prompt and careful publication of other categories of objects has made it possible for others to incorporate them into more general studies of artefacts and so to establish their context in the history of Palestinian and Near Eastern culture. The Megiddo volumes are, because of the sheer numbers of objects and the geographical factors alluded to in the previous chapter, a veritable gold-mine for such studies, and the time has now come for the process to be reversed and for this more general knowledge to be put to use in new detailed work on the history of Megiddo itself. Some studies of this kind have already appeared and have provided invaluable help in the preparation of the present, necessarily brief, account of the site. Much more remains to be done, as we shall observe at appropriate places, and advances in understanding can certainly be ex-pected, in particular, from the recent excavations at the neighbouring sites of Taanach and Tell Keimun (Jokneam).

## Recent Israeli excavations

In the meantime some further excavation on a small scale has been done under the auspices of the Institute of Archaeology at the Hebrew University of Jerusalem. This was initiated by Professor Yigael Yadin, who in 1960 had recently come to the end of four seasons of very extensive excavations at Hazor (Tell el-Qedaḥ) in the upper Jordan Valley. Yadin had already, in an article published in 1958, drawn attention to the similarity between the early Iron Age gates at Hazor and Megiddo and he had found in the plans of R. A. S. Macalister's early excavations at Gezer (1902–5, 1907–9) a structure which, by a brilliant conjecture, subsequently confirmed by excavation, he identified as one half of a third gate of the same period, with an almost identical plan to the other two. Thinking it strange that the gates at Hazor and Gezer were set in casemate walls while the gate at Megiddo was associated with a massive solid wall, Yadin undertook a brief investigation at Megiddo to test his theory that there too the gate in question (the so-called 'Solomonic' gate) was part of a casemate fortification system and at the same time to try to clarify other aspects of the history of Israelite Megiddo. It was an excellent example of what is called a 'problem-centred' excavation. Already after only a few days' work Yadin was able to report some startling discoveries. Beneath a stretch of the solid wall in the north-east of the tell, which the earlier excavators had left untouched, there was visible a line of fine masonry almost 30 metres long, which proved to be the outer north wall of a rectangular 'fort' of an earlier period. To the east and west of this building, but still under the solid wall, were a series of rooms which Yadin identified as casemates, and he quickly drew the conclusion that these were the fortifications that were to be associated with the Solomonic gate, so that the pattern of defence at Hazor, Gezer and Megiddo was essentially identical. The pottery found in his new excavations seemed to confirm this view and to show that the solid wall (with a later gate) represented the fortifications of the following century, probably constructed under King Ahab of Israel. Other structures found by the American expedition could be allocated to one of these two phases of Megiddo's history. Yadin's theory and alternatives to it are discussed more fully below, in Chapter 6 (see pp. 85–92). Later excavations (in 1966–7 and 1971–2) brought to light further details of the 'fort' and provided the opportunity to examine other features of the Israelite city, including the different protected approaches to the water sources. Trial excavations on the slopes of the terrace to the north of the tell showed that it was largely artificial and that it was used for burials in the early part of the Middle Bronze Age.

Some of Yadin's colleagues at the Hebrew University also made small probes in other parts of the site: in 1965 I. Dunayevsky investigated the

23

Bronze Age sacred area on the summit and as a result proposed new conclusions about the order and dates of the temples there, while in 1974 A. Eitan uncovered further remaiņs of an Iron Age public building on the eastern slopes, which had been touched by one of Loud's trenches. This he associated with other Iron Age structures on the slopes further to the south which had been found by Fisher and Guy.

## Further reading

On the general development of archaeological technique in Palestine see the companion volume to this one by P. R. S. Moorey, *Excavation in Palestine* (Guildford, 1982), ch.4.

The results of the major excavations at Megiddo have been published in a series of large volumes: G. Schumacher, *Tell el-Mutesellim I*, in two parts, text and plates (Leipzig, 1908); C. Watzinger, *Tell el-Mutesellim II* (Leipzig, 1929); R. S. Lamon, *The Megiddo Water System*, OIP XXXII (Chicago, 1935); H. G. May and R. M. Engberg, *Material Remains of the Megiddo Cult*, OIP XXVI (Chicago, 1935); P. L. O. Guy and R. M. Engberg, *Megiddo Tombs*, OIP XXXIII (Chicago, 1938) (the tombs found on the eastern slopes); R. S. Lamon and G. M. Shipton, *Megiddo I. The Seasons of 1925–34, Strata I–V*, OIP XLII (Chicago, 1939); G. Loud, *The Megiddo Ivories*, OIP LII (Chicago, 1939); G. Loud, *Megiddo II, Seasons of 1935–39*, OIP LXII, two parts, text and plates (Chicago, 1948). The Chicago reports are now available in microfiche from the University of Chicago Press.

Preliminary notices of Schumacher's work appeared in the *Mitteilungen und Nachrichten des DPV* between 1904 and 1906 and these provide some additional information. The preliminary reports of Fisher, *The Excavation of Armageddon* (Chicago, 1929), and Guy, *New Light from Armageddon* (Chicago, 1931), help with the background and policy of the excavation. Analyses of the pottery of the earlier strata from the Chicago excavations may be found in R. M. Engberg and G. M. Shipton, *Notes on the Chalcolithic and Early Bronze Age Pottery of Megiddo*, SAOC, 10 (Chicago, 1934) – this volume deals with the domestic occupation on the south-eastern slopes – and G. M. Shipton, *Notes on the Megiddo pottery of Strata VI–XX*, SAOC, 17 (Chicago, 1939).

For the Israeli excavations see Yadin's articles, 'New Light on Solomon's Megiddo', *BA* 23(1960), 62–8; 'Megiddo of the Kings of Israel', *BA* 33(1970), 66–96, 'Notes and News: Megiddo', *IEJ* 22(1972), 161–4; and ch.13 of his Schweich lectures for 1970, *Hazor: the Head of all those Kingdoms (Joshua 11:10)*, (London, 1972); I. Dunayevsky and A. Kempinski, 'The Megiddo Temples', *ZDPV* 89(1973), 161–87; A. Eitan, 'Notes and News: Megiddo', *IEJ* 24(1974), 275–6.

An excellent summary of the discoveries at the site can be found in M. Avi-Yonah and E. Stern (ed), *Encyclopaedia of Archaeological Excavations in the Holy Land* (Jerusalem, London and Englewood Cliffs, 1975–8), vol.3, pp. 830–56 (with bibliography). Additional bibliography is given in E. K. Vogel, *Bibliography of Holy Land Sites* (Cincinnati, 1971), and E. K. Vogel and B. Holtzclaw, *Bibliography of Holy Land Sites, Part II* (Cincinnati, 1982), both offprints from *Hebrew Union College Annual* (vols 42 and 52); and at the end of the remaining chapters of this book.

# 3

# The Earliest Settlements at Megiddo

## From Village to City

Megiddo was not, according to the evidence at present available, one of the first places in Palestine to see settled human occupation. The earliest identifiable remains come from Area BB of the American excavations and indicate a beginning of settlement in the later part of the Neolithic period, c.5000 BC. Some toothed sickle blades found in a cave in the bedrock (designated by the Americans as 'Stratum –XX') and potsherds with either an incised herringbone design or a painted decoration from the deposits that lay on the bedrock (Stratum XX, 1st phase) are characteristic of the Yarmukian culture of this period, as represented by the ancient site of Shaar haGolan, near the southern end of the Sea of Galilee. Our knowledge of these early levels is limited by the fact that only in two small areas, comprising together about 700 square metres, was bedrock reached on the tell, and similar if less severe limitations apply to the history of occupation in the following three millennia (5000–2000 BC), in other words to half the period during which the tell was inhabited. The American excavators reached these prehistoric levels in only one of their areas on the tell (BB) and in a small area on the south-eastern slopes below the tell, which the ancient settlers mainly used as a cemetery. Schumacher's main trench cut through the early deposits at one point, but his report provides little information about them. For this reason alone any account of the first stages of the history of Megiddo must be a tentative one. There is in addition intense discussion and controversy among archaeologists at present about the processes at work in Palestine as a whole during this period, so that no one theory can be regarded as a secure framework into which the fragmentary evidence from Megiddo might be fitted. In the following pages we shall therefore concentrate on a description of the main finds: those readers who wish to pursue the scholarly discussion may consult the works mentioned at the end of the chapter.

The Neolithic settlement was followed by a village of the Chalcolithic period whose remains have been found in Strata XX (2nd phase) and XIX on the tell and in 'Stages VII–IV' on the lower slopes. The area exposed on the

Plate 3    The Chalcolithic shrine seen from the north (G. I. Davies)

tell was at first occupied by small houses built of stone or mudbrick, with either a rounded or a rectangular plan, but in the later part of the period these were replaced by a temple with a paved courtyard and an enclosure wall extending to the east. The walls of the temple are still visible today (plate 3): the main room was four metres from front to rear and a little over twelve metres broad. A circular structure *c*.2.25 metres in diameter, perhaps an altar, was assigned by the excavators to the next higher stratum (XVIII), but it may have belonged to this shrine, as it is situated directly opposite its entrance. Some of the paving stones of the courtyard bore incised drawings of humans and animals (figure 4), as did some potsherds of this period. The pottery itself is of several different styles which are paralleled at other sites in different parts of Palestine. Some of it is characteristic of the Megiddo area, such as the grey-burnished 'Esdraelon Ware' and vessels with a striped or network pattern of decoration in brown, red or yellow ('grain wash'). Another type, with red burnish, occurs all over Palestine, including the important settlement at Jericho, while a further group belongs to the so-called 'Ghassulian' culture, which was for a time dominant in southern Palestine, including En-Gedi, where there was a shrine very similar to that described above. To deduce tribal movements from these varied contacts would be hazardous, but they suggest that Megiddo was at this time a place where a variety of cultural traditions were

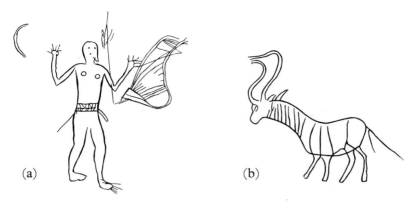

(a)                                                (b)

Figure 4   Drawings of (a) harpist and (b) horned animal incised on stones from the
courtyard of the Chalcolithic shrine (Stratum XIX). (*Megiddo II*, plate 273.5
and 276.12)

known, whether that came about through mixing of populations, trade or a combination of the two. In one respect Megiddo so far stands somewhat apart from the other Chalcolithic settlements: there is very little evidence of the use of metal.

The Chalcolithic village may be dated approximately to the second half of the fourth millennium BC: radiocarbon dates for Tomb A94 at Jericho, where the red-burnished pottery was found, support this dating. There are signs, both at Megiddo and elsewhere, that the Chalcolithic material culture continued to exist side-by-side with the new technical developments which mark the beginning of the Early Bronze Age. Indeed, according to Kathleen Kenyon's re-evaluation of the American excavation report, the village character of the settlement also remained unaltered in the first centuries of the third millennium. The massive circuit wall at the edge of the mound, which the excavators regarded as a city wall of Stratum XVIII (EB I), was interpreted by her as a retaining wall to support the terrace on which the large buildings of Strata XVII–XVI (EB II–III) were constructed, perhaps *c*.2700 BC. Two other large walls which join this wall are probably also part of this system of terracing. On this view the first Early Bronze Age settlement is represented in the excavated areas only by a few small buildings shown on the plan of Stratum XVIII and some contemporary remains on the lower slopes.

Even in the small area excavated the change from this modest settlement to the grand scale of the structures of Strata XVII-XVI is very apparent, and we may legitimately speak of it as a process of urbanisation. The terracing operations already referred to presuppose the availability of a large labour force and a substantial economic surplus, and this surely points to the rise of a complex and hierarchical structure within the population. On the new terrace a large building was constructed (3177), with a complicated layout of rooms and

27

Plate 4   Round altar of Early Bronze Age II (G. I. Davies)

courts and a stone-built drainage system of which a part has survived. The building is precisely aligned on the edges of what we have taken to be the retaining walls beneath. Between this building and some smaller buildings to the west there is a sharp rise in the floor level of about two metres, which probably indicates that a terrace wall also originally stood between them, although the excavators found only the remains of later walls here.

On the presumed higher terrace, behind the small buildings, stood a circular structure, which is still visible today, some eight metres in diameter and one and a half metres high, with a flight of steps leading up to the top on the south-east side (4017 – see plate 4). An enclosure wall was built around it, with an entrance apparently on the south-east. Within this wall there were large quantities of animal bones and broken pottery. This, together with the enclosure wall and the steps, identifies the structure as an open-air altar on which sacrifices were offered. There were very likely other cultic buildings in the vicinity at this time, just as there were later (see pp. 30–33), but the excavation was too restricted at this depth to expose them. Possibly the small rooms near the presumed upper terrace-wall were part of a temple precinct; at any rate the entrance to the altar enclosure was from this side. On the south side of the altar a street about one and a half metres wide led towards the centre of the city and some rectangular rooms were uncovered on each side of

28

Plate 5   Copper 'ceremonial sword' of Stratum XVIII (*Megiddo II*, plate 283.1)

it, though not enough to determine the plan and character of the buildings to which they belonged. Occupation also continued on the lower slopes till the end of the EB III period and remains of buildings were found here, as well as burials in caves and rock-cut chambers. From the later part of this period burials also began to be made within the city itself, but the total number of burials so far discovered from the Early Bronze Age is small, given the length of the period and the size of the town.

The pottery associated with Strata XVIII–XVI includes typical Early Bronze Age forms such as hole-mouth jars, stump-based jars and flat platters with low rims, and it reflects marked improvements in the technique of manufacture as compared with the pottery of the Chalcolithic period. The clay was better prepared, a primitive wheel began to be used and the use of a closed kiln made for higher temperatures and more even firing. The other small finds indicate that alongside artefacts of bone, flint and basalt, the Early Bronze Age inhabitants of Megiddo used copper tools and weapons. They included a chisel, a spatula, two pins, a socketed spearhead and what the excavators described as 'a ceremonial sword(?)' (plate 5). Although no axeheads were found, there were two moulds for their manufacture, one made of baked clay and the other of limestone. Also worthy of note are over a dozen crudely made animal figurines of clay, apparently representing cattle. Surprisingly little of a distinctive type of burnished pottery of northern origin ('Khirbet Kerak ware') has been found at Megiddo, compared with the quantities known from EB III levels at neighbouring sites such as Afula, Beth-shean and Khirbet Kerak itself. This has led some archaeologists to suppose that Megiddo was abandoned early in the EB III period or, alternatively, that it was for a time a centre of Egyptian influence in Canaan, opposed to the ambitions of those who used the 'Khirbet Kerak' pottery. Neither of these theories is likely to be correct. The pottery evidence as a whole suggests that Megiddo continued to be occupied to the end of EB III, but there is no evidence at present of Egyptian contacts there at this time. At most it may be justified to see Megiddo as

29

having remained largely aloof from the cultural and perhaps mercantile developments represented by the new pottery.

## Megiddo in a time of Economic and Political Decline

The period between the end of EB III and the beginning of the Middle Bronze Age (c.2300–2000) has been, as far as the whole of Palestine is concerned, a source of particularly severe disagreement among scholars for over a generation. This is reflected in the fact that it is currently referred to by no less than three different names – 'Middle Bronze Age I', 'Intermediate Early Bronze-Middle Bronze Period' and, with growing acceptance, 'Early Bronze Age IV' – which express different views about its connections (or lack of them) with the periods which precede and follow it. But scholars also disagree over whether its beginning and end were due to the arrival of a new population group or groups or, for example, to climatic changes; and over how (if at all) it is to be sub-divided chronologically. Here again I shall refrain from any account of the more general issues and concentrate on the evidence from Megiddo itself, which in certain respects contrasts with that from other sites. Whereas this period is elsewhere represented chiefly by tombs which contain pottery of much poorer quality than that of Early Bronze Age I–III (suggesting to some a nomadic population at this time), at Megiddo some impressive buildings, including temples, are found on the tell and the pottery includes some very fine decorated wares alongside the coarser types. This would seem to imply that Megiddo was less seriously affected than other places by the factors, whatever they were, which brought about this period of widespread political and economic decline.

In the western part of Area BB the buildings of Early Bronze Age II–III were replaced in Stratum XV by three more or less identical buildings, still visible on the site, which consisted of a rectangular room with an open area in front flanked by side walls which probably formed a porch (figure 5). There is some evidence that each also had a side room, perhaps for storage. They adjoin in the north and west the round stone altar built in Stratum XVII (above, p. 28), which already suggests a religious function for them, and this is confirmed by the rectangular platforms against the rear walls, opposite the entrance, of two of them (plate 6). These temples seem to represent a new development of the sacred area, but the ground beneath them has not yet been fully excavated, so that it must remain uncertain whether they were preceded by earlier temples. A few objects which could have been connected with the cult were found, but none which defines its character at all clearly.

30

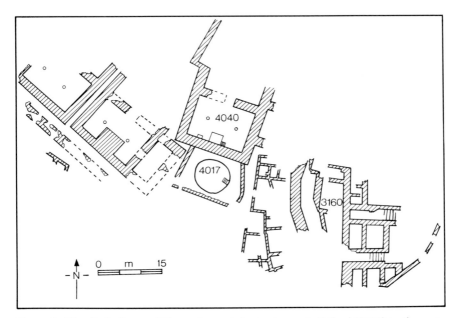

Figure 5 The Early Bronze IV temples and the 'staircase-building' (3160) to the east. The 'twin temples' are to the west of Temple 4040. (Andrew Brown; based on *Megiddo II*, figures 393–5)

The two westerly temples stand side-by-side, with parallel walls, and were undoubtedly built at the same time, perhaps for a god and his consort. Behind them is a thick wall, which may have surrounded the sacred precinct. The excavators' report gives no indication that the third temple (4040) was of a different date and the similar floor-levels of all three would support the view that they were all built at the same time. However, the third temple is oriented more to the north than the other two and actually obstructs the approach to the central temple. Kenyon therefore suggested that the two 'twin' temples were built first and were then replaced by the third temple. Her view has not gone unchallenged, and more evidence will be needed to resolve the issue conclusively. On the other hand the attribution of all three temples to Early Bronze IV (as I shall call this period) still seems the most likely view. It has been argued that they were built in EB III, but on very flimsy evidence. The pottery found in and around the temples is a mixture of EB II–III, EB IV and Middle Bronze I. The MB I pottery is almost entirely from tombs dug down from a later floor-level and can be disregarded. It is clear that the temples were in use in EB IV (for further evidence of this in relation to Temple 4040, see below) and the few EB II–III pieces could easily be intrusive.

The temples (and altar 4017, which remained in use) were not the only structures ascribed to Stratum XV. To the south-east a terrace-wall was found and beyond it, built over Building 3177 of Strata XVII–XVI, was a structure incorporating two staircases ascending the mound from the direction of the city wall. By means of these, it has been conjectured, a splendid access was provided to the temple area above. It remains something of a problem that they appear to lead to the back of the temples – though there could perhaps have been a processional way that led round to the north side – and it may be that this staircase-building (to which some walls marked on the plans of Strata XVI and XIV seem to belong) is from a secondary phase of Strata XVII–XVI. Unfortunately no pottery was reported from it, so its date cannot be definitely fixed.

In the later stages of EB IV only Temple 4040 remained in use, and its character was greatly changed. The large round altar to the south of it was abolished and a pavement was built over it. On this pavement (which was mistakenly ascribed to Stratum XIIIB in the report) was found a small deposit of clearly EB IV pottery, including a curious lamp with seven interconnecting cups. This pavement formed a raised open area behind Temple 4040, which may have been used for outdoor rites connected with the worship there. Inside the greater part of the main cult room was filled with rubble, leaving only a small walled *cella* in the centre between the entrance and the platform at the

Plate 6    Temple 4040 of Early Bronze IV from the north-east (G. I. Davies)

rear. These two changes seem to point to a move from a cult with a strongly public character and a long tradition (the round altar) to a much more enclosed style of worship, in which perhaps only a few priests participated. The date of this rebuilding of the temple is indicated by the fact that in the north wall there was found a fenestrated axehead of a kind which is typical of EB IV. Outside the temple there are also signs of rebuilding of this quarter of the city. The ceremonial gateway to the east went out of use and was replaced by a complex of small rooms.

The EB IV pottery from the temple area on the tell is of a kind which has chiefly been found in contemporary deposits in southern Palestine, for example at Lachish and Tell Beit Mirsim. The pottery from the tombs on the south-eastern slopes, however, is quite different. There is general agreement that the pottery of one of these tombs, T. 1101B–1102 Lower, stands apart from the other tombs of this period by its proximity to the styles of earlier centuries. In addition this tomb is not of the same very finely-hewn type as the others. It must be from the very beginning of EB IV, before the new features began to appear. The main group of tombs are of the 'shaft grave' type, of which about twenty-five were excavated by the American expedition. Others exhibiting the same method of construction and precisely similar types of pottery had been found by Schumacher in an area 250–350 metres south-west of the area cleared by the Americans, which shows that the cemetery was much more extensive than is usually supposed.

The common characteristic of all these tombs is the vertical shaft, square or circular in cross-section, by which access was gained to the burial chamber or chambers (figure 6). The shaft was normally about two metres deep and in some cases footholds are preserved in the sides. About a third of the tombs have a horizontal passage leading from the foot of the shaft to one side of a rectangular chamber, which has entrances to smaller chambers at a slightly higher level on its other three sides. Others have a smaller number of chambers or a different layout. The continuation of the practice of multiple burial at Megiddo and (to a lesser extent) in the similar tombs at Beth-shean marks an interesting difference from the almost contemporary graves at Jericho, which generally contained only a single burial. From the finds it appears that the people buried in these tombs used two different styles of pottery (figure 7). One is generally hand-made and characterised by a red slip or paint decoration and large ledge-handles. Jugs with wide, deep mouths, lug-handled jars and small, squat cups are common types. This kind of pottery has been found at such sites as Beth-shean and Tiberias and also east of the Jordan at el-Husn, and it can be related in various ways to Early Bronze I–III pottery. Alongside this there is another style of much finer, decorated pottery whose origin appears to lie in Syria. This is wheel-made and of a grey ware which is dec-

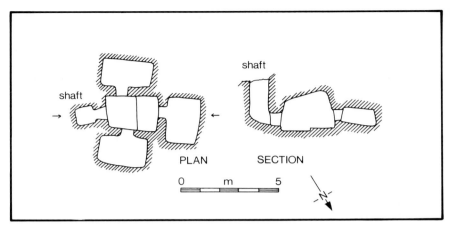

Figure 6 Plan of a four-chambered shaft tomb (T.878). (Andrew Brown; based on *Megiddo Tombs*, figure 42)

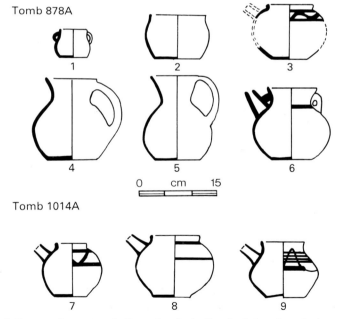

Figure 7 Pottery from two shaft tombs, including both hand-made (nos. 1 –2, 4–6) and 'grey ware' types (nos. 3, 7–9). (Andrew Brown; based on *Megiddo Tombs*, plates 20 and 22)

orated with yellowish bands, sometimes wavy, on the upper part of the vessel. Rounded cups and spouted jars ('teapots') are the most common types. While exact parallels to the decoration are few, two 'teapots' of the same shape and decoration were found at Yabrud, 60 km north-east of Damascus, and in general the shapes are so close to Syrian styles and so alien to Palestine that the Megiddo examples must be presumed to have come from Syria. Megiddo is by some way the most southerly of the sites at which this type of pottery has been found – a further pointer to its many contacts with the wider world. So far these types of pottery have not been found on the tell. At Hazor the decorated pottery was found in an area of dwellings, which suggests that evidence of related buildings may also be brought to light at Megiddo by further excavation on or around the tell. It is certainly hard to imagine that those who constructed such fine tombs for the dead did not also build houses for the living.

The mixture of locally-developed pottery styles with others of foreign origin may indicate that the group which buried its dead at Megiddo at this time was an indigenous group with trade links with inland Syria. It is possible, however, that they included families who were themselves immigrants from Syria and this seems to be confirmed by the burial customs. The regularity and excellence of the rock-cut chambers is unparalleled in the preceding period at Megiddo and the most telling comparisons are again with sites in central Syria such as Qatna. Burial practices are likely to have been conservative and it is reasonable to attribute the change to the arrival of new settlers. It is understandable that such newcomers should also employ the local pottery for everyday purposes.

In her widely-used textbook *Archaeology in the Holy Land* Kathleen Kenyon entitled the chapter which dealt with this period 'The Arrival of the Amorites'. 'Amorites' is a name used in the Old Testament to designate a people who lived in Canaan before the Israelites. Sometimes it appears to stand for the pre-Israelite population as a whole (e.g. Genesis 15:16), as an equivalent term to 'Canaanites', but elsewhere the Amorites are only one among several tribal groups who occupied the land in early times (e.g. Genesis 15:21). It was Kenyon's view that these Amorites were the direct descendants of newcomers who brought with them the material culture here under discussion. Emphasising its discontinuity from Early Bronze I–III, with its distinctive pottery and generally non-sedentary pattern of life, and its close links with Syria, she saw it as the more or less contemporary counterpart of the movement into Mesopotamia from the north-west of people who are variously called MAR.TU or Amurru in Babylonian texts. In these texts Amurru is sometimes an area in Syria, and so it seemed natural to suppose that it was from here that the biblical Amorites also came. Other archaeologists such as Nelson Glueck saw in this movement of people the historical context for the migration of Abraham and his family from Mesopotamia to Canaan (Genesis 12), and as a result it became commonplace to refer to this period as 'The Patriarchal Age'.

Recent research has cast doubt on these correlations between the Bible and archaeology in a number of ways. On the archaeological side, scholars are today much less ready than Kenyon was to attribute the EB IV material culture as a whole to invaders from the north and east. The very preference for the term 'EB IV' betokens a growing consensus that the inhabitants of Palestine at this time were, in the main, the descendants of those who had lived there for centuries past. Only a relatively small influx of newcomers is necessary to explain developments such as those which have been described above. On the other hand, both critical examination of the biblical text and more refined comparative studies have cast doubt on the view that the Hebrew patriarchs are to be seen as part of a great 'Amorite' migration. The parallels in customs cited by W. F. Albright and John Bright, for example, have proved in many cases not to be as close or as unique as was previously thought. It is now more generally accepted that the stories of the patriarchs are traditional literature to which many generations contributed, and as a result to associate these stories with one particular 'age' is less important than was once supposed.

*Further reading*

The primary evidence on which this chapter is based can be found in Loud, *Megiddo II* (Area BB), Engberg and Shipton, *Notes...*, Guy and Engberg, *Megiddo Tombs*, and Schumacher, *Tell el-Mutesellim I*, pp. 165–73 (tombs groups F and I): see p. 24 for publication details. On the archaeology and history of Palestine generally in this period see K. M. Kenyon, *Archaeology in the Holy Land*, 4th ed. (London and New York, 1979), pp. 43–147, and *The Cambridge Ancient History*, 3rd ed., I/1 (Cambridge, 1970), pp. 510–37, I/2 (Cambridge, 1971), pp. 208–37 and 567–94. Particular topics are dealt with by D. Ussishkin, 'The Ghassulian Shrine at En-Gedi', *Tel Aviv* 7(1980), 1–44; A. Ben-Tor, *Cylinder Seals of Third Millennium Palestine*, BASOR Supplement Series, 22 (Cambridge, Mass., 1978), pp. 101–9; I. Dunayevsky and A. Kempinski, *ZDPV* 89(1973), 161–87 (shrines); K. Kenyon, 'Some Notes on the Early and Middle Bronze Age Strata at Megiddo', *Eretz-Israel* 5(1958), 51*–60*; J. A. Callaway, 'New Perspectives on Early Bronze III in Canaan', in P. R. S. Moorey and P. J. Parr (eds), *Archaeology in the Levant. Essays for Kathleen Kenyon* (Warminster, 1978), pp. 46–58 (Egyptian involvement in Canaan); Kenyon, *Amorites and Canaanites*, Schweich Lectures for 1963 (London, 1966); E. Oren, *The Northern Cemetery of Beth-Shan* (Leiden, 1973); K. Prag, 'The Intermediate Early Bronze–Middle Bronze Age: An Interpretation of the Evidence from Transjordan, Syria and Lebanon', *Levant* 6(1974), 69–116 (also in *PEQ* 116(1984), 58–68); W. G. Dever, 'New Vistas on the EB IV ('MB I') Horizon in Syria-Palestine', *BASOR* 237(1980), 35–64 (includes surveys of the evidence and the scholarly discussion). On the 'Amorite' theory and the placing of the Hebrew patriarchs in this period see the chapters by W. G. Dever and W. M. Clark in J. H. Hayes and J. M. Miller (eds), *Israelite and Judaean History* (London, 1977).

# 4

# Canaanite Megiddo

According to the biblical book of Judges Megiddo was one of the last Canaanite cities to fall into Israelite hands (1:27–8). In all probability, along with Jerusalem to the south and the other great cities of the plain and valley of Jezreel, it remained essentially Canaanite until the reign of David (*c*.1000 BC). Here Canaanite civilisation survived as both an inspiration and an enticement to the Israelite tribes and, while the pre-eminent position of Jerusalem as a transmitter of Canaanite culture is not to be denied, it is likely that the contribution of Megiddo and its neighbours to the development of the northern tribes was no less important. For this reason alone a thorough examination of the archaeological evidence from Megiddo in the second millennium BC is of particular interest and long overdue. But in addition the evidence which is available, while by no means complete or without problems of interpretation, is so impressive in both its quantity and its richness that even after nearly fifty years it is still virtually without an equal in the contribution which it has to make to our knowledge and understanding of the Canaanite civilisation in Palestine. Besides the architectural remains and the wide range of artefacts found especially in the tombs, there is a substantial corpus of written texts which help to illuminate the history of the city. These include a number of Egyptian inscriptions found at the site itself, some letters sent by the king of Megiddo to the Egyptian court and, most vivid of all, the account in the annals of Tuthmosis III of his siege of Megiddo *c*.1468 BC, which is sometimes referred to as 'the first recorded battle in history'.

In archaeological terms this chapter will be concerned with Megiddo in the Middle and Late Bronze Ages and the first part of the Iron Age. The transitions between these periods do not correspond to sharp cultural or political changes at Megiddo: they are not marked by evidence of violent destruction or abandonment and there is a strong element of continuity both in the architecture and in the artefacts, such as pottery. There are changes, for example in burial practice, which may represent the arrival of new elements in the population and altered political circumstances, but the general impression is of a stable society enjoying considerable prosperity and able to absorb a variety of new ideas without fundamental change. We may refer to it as 'Canaanite' on the basis of the biblical term used for its final stages, even though this name does not seem to have been generally used before the fifteenth century BC.

The evidence to be considered comes mainly from Strata XIII–VI of the American excavations, but also from some tombs on the slopes and certain of Schumacher's discoveries. In addition to Area BB in the east of the mound, the excavations in Area AA in the north now have much to contribute to our account, and to a lesser extent this is also true of Area CC in the south and Area DD in the north-east. The unsatisfactory analysis and recording of the stratification continue to pose problems, which are increased by the large numbers of burials within the city walls at this time and by disturbances due to building operations of both this and later periods, particularly in the eastern part of the mound. Kenyon, in an article published in 1969, endeavoured, by a classification of the pottery found in the tombs within the city, to establish a firmer basis for the understanding of its architectural development. But, strange as it may seem in view of her general emphasis on stratigraphy, her ideas about the sequence of pottery types (which she related to the tombs, but not the tell, at Jericho) were based on *a priori* assumptions about the relationship between different groups and come into conflict at various points with the actual structural sequence on the tell. Some of her conclusions still seem valid, but the material is in need of a fresh evaluation which would combine Kenyon's skill in salvaging useful information from old excavation reports with the growing data from more recent excavations of stratified deposits from the second millennium, such as those at Aphek (Ras el-Ain), Gezer and Lachish.

## The renewal of city life (Middle Bronze I)

In Middle Bronze Age I Temple 4040 in the eastern area of excavation, with some rooms adjoining it on the south, continued in use, thus providing an indication of some continuity, in religion at least, with the preceding era. It was surrounded on all sides by burials of the period, which had been dug into the ruins of earlier houses. Kenyon was inclined to think that this was the full extent of the remains from Middle Bronze I (her phase J), but it is also necessary to attribute to this period some structures in the vicinity of the temple (shown on the plans of Strata XIIIB and XIIIA), which she dated to the beginning of Middle Bronze II. Even more impressive evidence comes from Area AA. Here the plan of Stratum XIII (figure 8) shows a brick-built city gate with a stepped approach from outside the city ascending parallel to the wall and then turning at right angles to pass through a gatehouse. The city wall itself is 1.80 metres thick, with buttresses on its outer side and a limestone glacis on

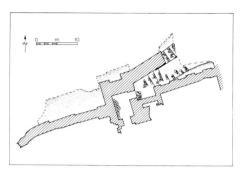

Figure 8 City wall and gate in Area AA (Stratum XIII), probably built *c*. 1850 BC. The dotted areas outside the wall mark the glacis. (Andrew Brown; based on *Megiddo II*, figure 378)

the slope of the mound beneath. Built against the inside of the wall is a Middle Bronze I tomb (T.4112), which indicates a lower chronological limit for the fortifications here. Theoretically they could belong to an earlier period (even the Early Bronze Age has been suggested), but this is unlikely in view of the fact that they were certainly enlarged and reused in Middle Bronze II. There is a close resemblance between the buttresses here and those of the wall shown on the Stratum XIIIA plan of Area BB, and it seems likely that both are part of one and the same fortification system, belonging to a late phase of Middle Bronze I. The earlier phase(s), so far as we can tell (the excavations did not reach it in Area AA), was unfortified.

In several ways the beginning of the Middle Bronze Age represents a new departure in the material culture of Megiddo. As already indicated, burials become normal on the summit of the tell. The cemetery on the slopes contains only a few tombs from this period, but some more were found by Yadin in his excavations on the 'northern terrace'. The pottery is wholly wheel-made and characterised by a burnished dark red slip: both the decoration and some of the new forms which appear may be intended to recall metal prototypes. Perhaps most significant of all, it is at this time that bronze begins to replace copper as the material of tools and weapons, a change which presupposes both a technological step forward and wider trading connections giving access to tin, whose ultimate source, east of Mesopotamia, remains unknown. (In the early eighteenth century BC we have evidence in the Mari texts for the transfer of tin to Hazor and Laish (later Dan) in northern Palestine.) New forms of dagger (with a grooved blade) and axehead (with a notch, probably to aid binding to the haft) made from casts appear at this time. The evidence of Egyptian tomb-paintings, according to G. Posener, also suggests changes in

39

the style of clothes and hair-dressing in Palestine about now. In general there is throughout the land a gradual reversion to the urban settlements typical of Early Bronze I–III, in contrast to most of what we know of EB IV. There is ample justification in these innovations for the terminology used by Kenyon, Dever and in the present book, which makes the Middle Bronze Age begin at this point. They are not short-lived changes, but affect the local life-style for centuries to come.

But are they to be attributed to a new population becoming dominant at Megiddo and elsewhere? Or can they be explained by reference to factors like climatic change, the development of trade and consequent greater prosperity? The former explanation has enjoyed considerable popularity, and the change in burial practice may be particularly significant. If it is accepted, the origin of the new population becomes a subject for investigation and there has been wide agreement that a source in Syria, whether on the coast (Kenyon) or inland (Dever) should be envisaged. More recently, as for other cultural changes, it has become fashionable to point out how the new forms could have evolved from corresponding features in the local culture in the preceding period, with or without the stimulus of new trading links (J. N. Tubb). Megiddo at first sight looks like a prime candidate for local development since, unlike many other sites, it was more or less continuously occupied through Early Bronze IV. Yet on further examination the contrast with what immediately preceded is no less here than it is at other sites, so that continuity of development is not at all obvious. One discipline that might have something to contribute to this discussion is physical anthropology, which is able in some cases to distinguish different racial types by their skeletal characteristics, especially skull shape. According to Aleš Hrdlicka, who examined the skulls found in the tombs on the south-eastern slopes at Megiddo, there was a clear distinction between those of the Early Bronze Age, which were of a 'Mediter-ranean' type, and those of the Middle and Late Bronze Ages, which were shorter and broader, approximating to the 'Alpine' type. Only two skulls, both fragmentary, were available for the Middle Bronze Age, but both came from a tomb of MB I date, so they cannot be attributed to the effect of some later migration.

However the new urban phase in Palestine came about, it quickly came into contact with the revived power of Middle Kingdom Egypt, to judge from the 'Execration Texts', which probably date from the latter part of the nineteenth century BC. Two collections have been found, one earlier than the other, which are inscribed respectively on bowls and small statuettes. In each case the objects were intended for ritual smashing as a way of invoking disaster on Egypt's enemies. The names in the two collections include many localities in Palestine and their rulers and appear to indicate that between the writing of

Plate 7    Part of an inscribed statuette of the Egyptian official Thuthotep, found in the Late Bronze Age temple but to be dated *c*. 1900 BC (*Megiddo II*, plate 265)

the earlier and the later texts Palestine was being quite rapidly urbanised, with individual city-states increasingly being governed by a single ruler. This corresponds well to the transition at Megiddo during Middle Bronze I from the loose-knit first phase(s) to the well-fortified city of the later phase. In addition the autobiography of one Khu-sebek reports a campaign of Sesostris III of Egypt (*c*.1878–43) against the 'Asiatics', which reached 'a foreign country whose name was Sekmem' (*ANET*, p. 230): this is probably Shechem in central Palestine. Megiddo itself seems not to be named in any of these texts, but this could be due to the friendly relations which existed between it and the Egyptian court. Evidence of such contacts exists in parts of three black stone statuettes of a clearly Egyptian style (plate 7), which derive from this period and later suffered the indignity of being built into the altar-platform of the temple of Stratum VIIA at Megiddo (see below, p. 61). One of them bore a hieroglyphic inscription which begins:

An offering which the king gives (to) Khnum, Lord of the-Foreign-Country-of-the-God, that he may give an invocation-offering (consisting of) bread, beer, [cattle], fowl etc. to the *ka* of the [revered one], the Count, Controller of the Two Thrones, Overseer of Priests, Chief of Five, Royal Intimate, he who sees the mysteries of [the house of] the king and exalts the courtiers, the Great Overlord of [the Hare Nome] . . . [Thut]hotep, born to Si[t-Kheper-ke].

The titles are those of a high priest of the god Thoth and nomarch of a district in central Egypt, who is known from his tomb-inscription at el-Bersheh to have been a prominent official during the nineteenth century BC. The discovery of this inscription may imply that Thuthotep was stationed for a time

41

Plate 8    Middle Bronze Age II bone inlays (*Megiddo II*, plate 193.9)

at Megiddo, perhaps in some kind of ambassadorial role. A less specific indication (in terms of date) of Egyptian interest in Megiddo during Middle Bronze I may be provided by a scarab seal which is inscribed: 'Head of the bureau of the cattle census, Yufseneb'. This was found in a tomb of Middle Bronze II, but according to the Egyptologist J. A. Wilson both the name and the title are attested elsewhere only in the Egyptian Middle Kingdom, which corresponds closely in time to the Middle Bronze I period in Palestine. It may have been an heirloom, deriving ultimately from an Egyptian resident in Megiddo. On a less official level the Tale of Sinuhe (*ANET*, pp. 18–20) and the Satire on the Trades (*ANET*, p. 433) provide further evidence that Egyptian travellers were a not uncommon sight in Palestine at this time.

## A City of Palaces and Kings (Middle Bronze II)

The transition from MB I to MB II is now thought to fall around the middle of the eighteenth century BC. It corresponds to a time when Egypt was entering the 'Second Intermediate Period', a period extending to the middle of the sixteenth century during which the power of the native Egyptian rulers was first divided among rival dynasties and then (*c.*1650) largely taken over by rulers of foreign origin who formed the Fifteenth Dynasty. These came to be known as the 'Hyksos' (Egyptian *ḥḳꜣ ḫswt*), 'Rulers of foreign countries' (the term does not mean, as Josephus (following Manetho) thought, 'Shepherd Kings'). During this time of Egyptian weakness, from which no Egyptian texts referring to Palestine survive, the city-states of Palestine, and Megiddo among them, flourished as never before. It is common to refer to this as 'the Hyksos period' in Palestine, but this expression is best avoided, both because the period only partly overlaps with the period of Hyksos rule in Egypt in the strict sense and because it implies that we know more than in fact we do about the political relationship between Egypt and Palestine at this time.

According to the interpretation of the evidence given above, Megiddo had already been fortified in the later part of Middle Bronze Age I. Its defences were maintained and indeed strengthened in the following two centuries. In Area AA (Stratum XII) the gate described earlier now went out of use and a new city-wall was built over it. Soon afterwards there is evidence of a strengthening of the city-wall both here and in Area BB (where there was also a tower) by the construction against its outer face of an additional wall which doubled its thickness. Within the city too there are new buildings. Three adjoining houses were built against the city wall in Area AA, probably with a street in front of them running parallel to the wall (such a street was certainly in existence in Stratum X). Similar houses appear near the wall in Area BB (Stratum XII, Kenyon's phases M and N), with clear evidence of a street parallel to the wall.

Further to the west, beyond the site previously occupied by Temple 4040, the American expedition found part of a much more substantial building with walls 1.50–2.00 metres thick. This lay at the very edge of Schumacher's deep north–south trench and a fresh study of the plans drawn by Schumacher made it possible to recognise that it was the eastern wing of what Schumacher had termed the *Nordburg* or 'North Fortress'. This was an approximately rectangular building at least 35 metres long from north to south with rooms apparently arranged around a central court. Beneath it Schumacher had detected walls whose haphazard layout is reminiscent of the Middle Bronze I houses found nearby by the Americans. Very little work has been done on Schumacher's reports since the American excavations, but this correlation does provide an important clue for the interpretation of Schumacher's considerable finds in this area. Immediately to the south of the *Nordburg* and at virtually the same level lay a somewhat smaller complex of rooms which he called the *Mittelburg* ('Central Fortress'). Though less impressive in scale it is in some ways more interesting than the *Nordburg* because of some tombs underneath it which had survived intact and unopened, no doubt because of their subterranean location. Schumacher tells how the existence of one of the chambers was suspected from the hollow ring of a pick striking the stones, but was confirmed only when a stone was removed and a worker fell through the hole! Burial within the city walls and indeed below the floors of houses was common at Megiddo throughout the Middle Bronze Age, as it was at the neighbouring cities of Taanach and Afula, but tombs of the size and splendour of the largest of these were found nowhere else on the site, and there is therefore a strong presumption that, as Watzinger suggested in 1929, this was a

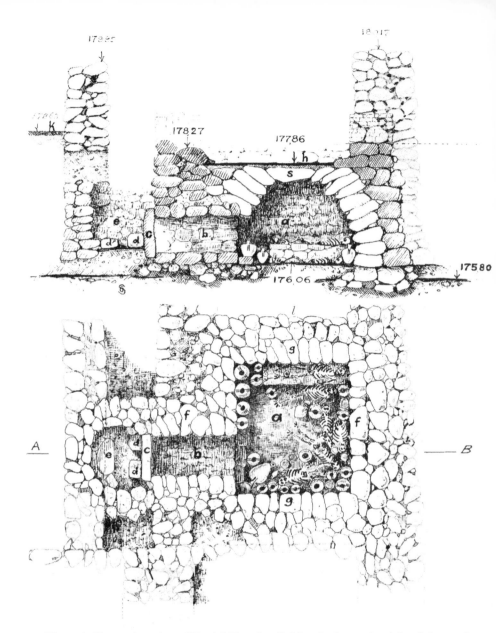

Figure 9  Plan and section of 'Burial Chamber I'. Note in the section (*above*) the crude vaulting of the roof of the underground chamber, and the skeletons and accompanying pottery marked on the plan (*below*). (G. Schumacher, *Tell el-Mutesellim I*, Tafel V)

mausoleum for a prince or king of Megiddo who had the *Nordburg* built as his palace.

One chamber ('Burial Chamber I') had internal dimensions of *c.* 2.60 metres by 2.15 metres and was covered by a vaulted stone roof showing a remarkably advanced technique for this early period (figure 9). According to Schumacher's calculations it was carrying a weight of 135 tons of overlying debris prior to his excavations without showing any signs of collapse. Entrance to the tomb was by a shaft descending from above on the east and a horizontal passage, which was closed at its outer end by a flat slab of limestone. Inside lay six undisturbed skeletons, five on the floor and one, a man, on a bench *c.* 40 cm high which extended along most of the north side of the chamber. With the latter were a variety of adornments, including several scarabs mounted in gold, dating from the Egyptian Middle Kingdom and therefore to be seen as heirlooms. Presumably this was the king or prince, while the other skeletons, two adult females, two adult males and one young male, belonged to members of his family or entourage. One of the women was laid beside the bench and may have been his wife. They were well supplied with provision for their journey into the afterlife, for no less than forty-two storage jars, large and small, were buried with them and in several of these were the remains of food, including cow and sheep bones and 'yellow remains of a milky liquid which had thickened into a hard mass', perhaps honey. In addition there were many bowls, platters and jugs, most of whose shapes point to a Middle Bronze II date for the burials. This is confirmed by the appearance of bone inlays, probably used to decorate small boxes, which were fashionable at Megiddo at just this time, as other burials on the tell and the slopes show (plate 8).

The other tomb beneath the *Mittelburg* ('Burial Chamber II') is much smaller (maximum internal dimensions 1.20 metres by 1.15 metres). The stonework is cruder but again the roof is vaulted, with a single very large stone acting as a keystone. It has a hole in the middle which could, if accessible from above, have been used to inspect the corpses and make further provisions of food for the deceased. The tomb contained the remains of twelve skeletons, piled on the southern part of the floor. Some wore bronze anklets, and a large storage jar and other vessels lay by each skull. Again there are some clear Middle Bronze II pottery types, which indicate when the burials began to be made, but the presence of some later forms shows that these tombs remained accessible down into Late Bronze Age I. Possibly gifts of food continued to be made for generations to the deceased. This grave is typical of many on the tell in the Middle Bronze Age, but none of the others seems to have contained as many as twelve skeletons. Perhaps it was the continuing existence of the palace, while the smaller surrounding houses were often being rebuilt, which led to such large numbers of burials being made in the same tomb.

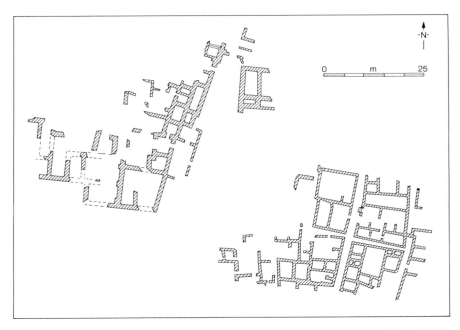

Figure 10 The eastern quarter of Megiddo (Stratum X) towards the end of the Middle Bronze Age showing the extension to the palace on the left and the new outer block of houses on the far right. (Andrew Brown; based on *Megiddo II*, figure 400)

Returning to the discoveries made by the American expedition, where the sequence of the structures is clearer, we can detect later in Middle Bronze Age II a two-stage enlargement of the palatial building (Kenyon's phases O and P, Strata XI–X). These alterations must reflect a growth in the power of the king and, as a direct consequence, an expansion of his entourage. In the east of Area BB the private houses continue, though the rooms are in several cases larger, perhaps forming open courtyards, and the line of the city wall must have been moved outwards, as a new block of houses was built over the wall described earlier (figure 10). The outermost rooms of this block and the city wall itself no longer survive in this area, having presumably collapsed through erosion down the slope. The fortifications of this period are, however, preserved in Area AA and are particularly interesting (Stratum XI, Kenyon phase AD). Here too the line of the wall was pushed out (by about eight metres), though in this case the purpose seems not to have been to accommodate a larger population, as the newly incorporated area was not used to build new houses: it may for a time have been an open space. What is more important about this new wall is the fact that it stands on a man-made earthen bank, which raised it some five metres above the existing slope of the mound. At Megiddo nothing similar had been undertaken since the Early Bronze Age (Stratum XVII–p. 27), but similar earthworks were constructed at many sites, such as Jericho, Shechem and Lachish, during Middle Bronze Age II and at Hazor the ramparts are particularly impressive, because they were built not on an already existing slope but on a flat surface. As elsewhere the artificial slope at Megiddo was protected by a glacis. Only the foundations of the wall itself survive, and they are peculiar in two respects. The wall is unusually narrow for a city wall (approximately 1.50 metres across), and every two metres or so there is a buttress on the inner side which projects about 1.50 metres. Undoubtedly these were intended to strengthen the otherwise very weak defences, and it is even possible that above ground level the space between the buttresses was filled with mud-bricks so as to make a wall of more regular thickness. Another possibility that merits consideration is that by this time Megiddo's strength was such or the danger of hostile attack so slight that its ruler thought that a token defensive wall was sufficient. At the eastern extremity of Area AA the wall abuts against a massive structure which appears to be the western half of a city gate.

The houses in Area AA at first show little change after the construction of the new wall, except that a structure connected with the presumed city gate encroaches on the easternmost house. But in the later part of Middle Bronze Age II first this house and its neighbour and then part of a third house are superseded by a large building of a quite new plan with a court at the centre (Strata X–IX, Kenyon's phases AF and AG). Its construction must be connected with a wholesale re-planning of this part of the city, as it is built over part of the city gate mentioned above. There continued to be important buildings on this site for some five hundred years (until Stratum VIIA). It is scarcely at this stage a royal palace, since that function seems more likely to have belonged to the *Nordburg* complex in the centre of the mound. Possibly its position in the area which was, because of the easy descent to the terrace below, usually the location of the main city gate can help to establish its significance, for it is likely that the city's military commander would have his headquarters near the city gate. The only difficulty with this is that it is not absolutely certain that there was a gate in this area at the time corresponding to Strata X–IX. As was noted above, the new plan abolished part of the city gate of the preceding period. It was the view of Loud that the strongly built gate a little to the east belonging to Sratum VIII may have already existed in Strata X–IX. But the alignment of this gate is different from that of the palace and the connection between them does not give the impression that they are parts of a defence system designed at one and the same time. Possibly, as Kenyon thought, the

gateway at this stage lay a little higher up the mound beyond the area excavated and the approach to it passed along the east wall of the palace, which is
of city-wall thickness, at least in Stratum IX. If this palace was actually in a
more forward position than the city gate, this would of course add weight to
the theory that it was connected with military activities.

The pottery from these levels (discounting intrusive pieces from later
tombs) is of the types characteristic of the later part of the Middle Bronze Age
in Palestine. The burnished red slip typical of MB I becomes less frequent.
Special mention should be made of the hand-made but finely decorated
pottery imported from Cyprus and Syria, which indicates the growing international trade links at this time. As is often the case, it is the tombs which have
preserved some of the most precious items (plate 9). Gold jewellery was found
still in place on some of the skeletons – headbands, ornate earrings, bracelets –
as well as beads and small jars of alabaster and faience, which point to some
commercial contact with Egypt. The Megiddo tombs bear witness to
considerably greater wealth than the comtemporary tombs from inland Jericho:
Megiddo's position ensured that it reaped an abundant harvest from trade as
well as agriculture. Items of bronze are also numerous and include arrowheads, socketed spearheads, daggers, knife-blades, chisels, toggle-pins (now
with ribbed or spiral decoration), needles and some crudely made figurines in
human form. Further light is shed on everyday life at this time by a number of
(unmarked) stone balance weights and a large set of twenty-six pierced clay
loom weights found in the domestic quarter of Area BB. Some similar weights
are stamped with impressions from a scarab seal: this is surprising, as they
cannot have been worth much.

One subject on which there is comparatively little information available at
present is the religion of Megiddo in the later part of the Middle Bronze Age.
Given the tendency for sacred sites to persist through long periods, it would be
expected that Temple 4040, which survived into Middle Bronze I, would have
been immediately followed by a new temple. According to a number of scholars this did indeed happen, for they believe that Temple 2048 (which will be
described later in the chapter: see pp. 60–3) or a predecessor of almost identical
plan to it was built in the Middle Bronze Age, like a very similar temple at Shechem. The comparison between the two structures was already being made in
the 1930s and in the Oriental Institute in Chicago there is an interesting letter
written in 1939 by Ernst Sellin, the Austrian excavator of Shechem, in which
he gave his view of the Shechem structure for the benefit of the American expedition. Despite the similarity of the plan, Loud felt compelled to ascribe
Temple 2048 to the Late Bronze Age and Kenyon presented additional stratigraphical arguments in 1969 which strongly support this view. The foundations of Temple 2048 are separated from the ruins of Temple 4040 by

Plate 9    Gold and faience jewellery from tombs of the end of the Middle Bronze Age
and the beginning of the Late Bronze Age (*Megiddo II*, plate 225.2, 3, 6
and 7)

deposits between 1.5 and 2 metres thick. No evidence remains of any building
in this area from the intervening period. On the plan of Stratum XII a number
of upright stone slabs occupied the area south of the site of Temple 4040.
Another group of similar slabs at a higher level is shown on the Stratum IX
plan at the centre of the 'rubble pavements' which lie beneath the foundations
of the Late Bronze Age temple. There may have been an enclosed shrine here
of which all evidence has disappeared, but it is possible that the whole area
was occupied by an open-air sanctuary in which the worship centred on standing stones like those which the excavators recorded. It is worth recalling that
the line of much larger standing stones at Gezer has now been firmly dated to
the end of the Middle Bronze Age, and the Megiddo stones may represent a
similar kind of cult on a smaller scale. In a locus of Stratum X (2032), a short
distance to the east of the sacred area, a number of peculiar decorated vessels
were found which are probably of a cultic character, as well as what may be a
small bronze snake. This, together with deposits of animal bones mixed with
pottery typical of Strata X–IX, strongly suggests that a sacrificial cult was
practised here.

## The 'Bichrome Ware' of Late Bronze Age I

The end of the Middle Bronze Age is conventionally placed c.1550 BC, close to
the time of the 'expulsion of the Hyksos' from Egypt. Culturally and architec-
turally the transition to the Late Bronze Age is barely discernible at Megiddo,
as there is considerable continuity with the preceding phase. Nor is there any
indication of disruption on the political level at this time. Nevertheless the
events of the mid-sixteenth century BC were in due course to be of great significance for the history of Palestine, and for Megiddo in particular, and it is
possible with hindsight to see that the first hundred years of the Late Bronze Age
were a period in which considerable upheavals were under way. Sharuhen in

49

the far south of Palestine was captured by Amosis, the founder of the Eighteenth Dynasty (*c*.1552–27 BC: see *ANET*, pp. 233–4) and several of his successors probably passed through Palestine, so that the destructions attested by archaeological evidence about this time at Hazor, Jericho, Lachish, Tell Beit Mirsim and Shechem could, in some cases at least, have been the result of Egyptian attacks. Literary evidence of such activity is however lacking. At Megiddo, the picture is one of continuing prosperity. The *Nordburg* and *Mittelburg* remained in existence. The blocks of houses in the south-east of Area BB were slightly modified (we follow here Kenyon's view that the very similar plans of this area in Strata IX, VIII and VIIB – apart from Temple 2048 – all relate to the late sixteenth and early fifteenth centuries). The situation in Area AA is very unclear and Kenyon's suggestion that the remains from this period were removed in an extensive rebuilding of this part of the city in the fourteenth century may well be correct. An alternative possibility is that the buildings of Stratum IX remained in existence through the first century of the Late Bronze Age.

The most distinctive feature of this rather obscure period is a very fine type of decorated pottery which has come to be known as 'Bichrome Ware'. This comprises mainly jugs, kraters and jars of a rather squat profile, finely made on the wheel from well-prepared clay (cf. figure 11). The decoration, which normally occupies the upper part of the vessel only, consists of a frieze bounded above and below by alternate bands of red and black paint. The frieze is generally divided into sections by vertical bands (often incorporating a geometrical design) and in each section there is a painting of a bird, a fish or some other kind of animal. In some cases the decoration is purely geometrical. At Megiddo this style of pottery has been found in Strata X, IX and VIII as well as in some tombs on the slopes, but the examples from Stratum X are all from tombs which (as is often the case) were dug into that level from above by the people of Stratum IX or later. Significant quantities of it also occur at Hazor and at Tell el-Ajjul south of Gaza, and some examples of it have been noted at many other sites, especially on the coast. Outside Palestine it has been found, for instance, at Ras Shamra (Ugarit), in Cyprus and in Egypt.

Not surprisingly, the origin of this fine pottery has been much discussed. Already in the 1930s it was being suggested that the close correspondence between its decorative motifs and those on some pottery found at Tell Billah in Mesopotamia justified its attribution to a Hurrian element in the population of Palestine, of whose presence there are clear indications in texts from the fifteenth and fourteenth centuries. This theory was given its fullest and most cogent expression by C. Epstein in 1966. Another view that was put forward before the Second World War was that the remarkable uniformity of the decoration pointed to its being the product of a single vase-painter working, it was suggested, at Tell el-Ajjul, from where it was exported widely in the Near East. In a modified form this view was also maintained by Ruth Amiran, who thought in terms of a school of painters (and potters) rather than a single individual and envisaged its location at 'one of the centres on the coast of Greater Canaan'. In the past ten years study of this question has been turned in an entirely new direction by the use of neutron activation analysis to determine the chemical composition of the clays out of which the bichrome ware is made. The result was to show that the great majority of the vessels from sites other than Megiddo were made of Cypriote clay and were presumably therefore produced in Cyprus itself, probably at Milia. Analysis of the pieces from

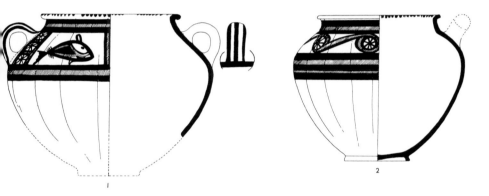

Figure 11  Bichrome pottery from Megiddo (*Megiddo II*, plate 53.1–2)

Megiddo showed, however, that while nine pieces were of Cypriote origin fourteen others were not, but had a chemical composition close to that of the local undecorated pottery from the site. Stylistic and material differences between the two groups could also be observed. It thus appears that the bichrome pottery was being made at or near to Megiddo, apparently to imitate the Cypriote originals and ensure that local potters benefited from the popularity of this presumably quite expensive ware.

## 'The capturing of Megiddo is the capturing of a thousand towns': the attack of Tuthmosis III

For the history of Megiddo in the fifteenth and fourteenth centuries BC we are in the unusual position of possessing written evidence in some quantity. By far the most extensive of these texts and from a historical point of view certainly

51

the most important are a group of Egyptian inscriptions of Tuthmosis III (1490–1436) which recount the events of his first Asiatic campaign (c.1468 BC). The longest and most detailed of these inscriptions, the Annals inscribed on the walls of the temple of Amun at Karnak, declares that all Palestine north of the Egyptian garrison in Sharuhen, 'from Iursa(Tell Jemmeh?) to the outer ends of the earth' was in revolt (*ANET*, p. 235). The initiative for this 'revolt' apparently came from further north, for the force which confronted Tuthmosis was led by 'that wretched enemy of Kadesh', the king of Kadesh (Tell Nebi Mend) on the Orontes, and included not only rulers from Palestine who had previously been 'loyal' to Egypt (i.e. on good terms with her) but contingents from far-off kingdoms like Naharin, Kode and possibly Mitanni. Tuthmosis had succeeded to the throne as a boy, but for over twenty years he had been overshadowed by his step-mother Hatshepsut, who apparently died or fell from power shortly before this campaign. It is possible that the energetic young king seized control from her precisely so as to deal with a situation in Palestine which must have seemed increasingly threatening to Egyptian interests. There is little doubt that the organised hostility to Egypt was due to the movement into Palestine of Hurrian groups from the north with a chariot-owning aristocracy, who were established in a leading role in many cities in the fifteenth century.

The Annals briefly report Tuthmosis' progress to the frontier post of Tjaru (Sile), near modern El Kantara, on to Gaza and then up the coastal plain to Yehem, which must have been near Tell el-Asawir on the southern slopes of the Carmel ridge. A stele found at Armant suggests that Tuthmosis may have met with some opposition on his journey through the plain (*ANET*, p. 234; cf. pp. 22–3 and 242–3). At Yehem there took place the famous council of war. It was known by this time that the enemy had congregated at Megiddo, and Tuthmosis evidently intended to march through the Carmel hills by way of Wadi Ara, which was the normal and most direct route. His senior officers were, however, reluctant to go by 'this road which becomes so narrow' and urged instead that the army should follow one of two alternative routes, which came out at Taanach and somewhere north of Megiddo. The description of the 'narrow' road which they gave matches exactly the conditions in the northern part of the Wadi Ara pass, as was shown in detail by H. H. Nelson. The two alternative routes proposed by Tuthmosis' officers can also be identified with some certainty on the assumption that they offered a safer approach to Megiddo. The route which comes out at Taanach is probably one which passes round the south of the Carmel hills by way of the plain of Arrabeh and Jenin. This is a much more open route which was a popular alternative to Wadi Ara in the nineteenth century. The route 'to the north side of Djefti', which came out north of Megiddo, is likely to be the pass (like Wadi Ara a chalk valley) which reached the plain of Esdraelon at Tell Keimun, some 14 km north of Megiddo. Militarily the advantage of both these routes was that they would allow the Egyptians to reach the open spaces of the plain at some distance from Megiddo and deploy their army in full strength before engaging the enemy. The only advantage of the more direct route would be surprise, but this could scarcely be relied upon. Nevertheless Tuthmosis stuck to his original choice, fearing (we are told by the court annalist) above all things that he might be thought a coward by his enemies, and announced that he would lead the army through the pass himself.

After a day spent making preparations the army set out on the march of some 20 km to Megiddo. It took two days to get the army through the pass and the annalist records, if the restoration of the text is correct, that they did not meet a single enemy soldier on their way. The alliance had drawn up its forces in the plain: '[their] southern wing was in Taanach, [while their] northern wing was on the south side . . .' (*ANET*, p. 236). Since the Armant stele says that the enemy were gathered at the mouth of the pass, the missing words at the end must have referred either to this (elsewhere it is called the Qina Valley) or, as seems more likely, to Megiddo itself. The king of Kadesh evidently did not know by what route the Egyptians were approaching and was guarding both the approach from the south-east and the exit from the pass. Tuthmosis was tempted to make an immediate attack, once the vanguard of his army was clear of the pass, but on this occasion he was persuaded to take the more cautious course and await the arrival of his whole army. As a result the battle was delayed until the next day (or even, if we take the date given in the Annals at face value, until the day after):

> Year 23, 1st month of the third season, say 21, the day of the feast of the *true* new moon. Appearance of the king at dawn. Now a charge was laid upon the entire army to *pass by* . . . His majesty set forth in a chariot of fine gold, adorned with his accoutrements of combat, like Horus the Mighty of Arm, a lord of action like Montu, the Theban, while his father Amon made strong his arms. The southern wing of his majesty's army was at a hill south of [the] Qina [*brook*], and the northern wing was to the northwest of Megiddo, while his majesty was in their center, Amon being the protection of his person (in) the melee and the strength of [*Seth pervading*] his members. (*ANET*, p. 236)

The Egyptian army was spread out to the west and south of Megiddo, its left wing having apparently moved north into the hollow that separates the tell and the ridge to its south from the hills behind (see figure 12). It must be presumed that the enemy, seeing the danger of being cut off from Megiddo and anxious to prevent the city from falling into Egyptian hands, had fallen back on the slopes north of the Qina brook (Wadi el-Lejjun). This would have been an excellent defensive position, had it not been for the move north by the

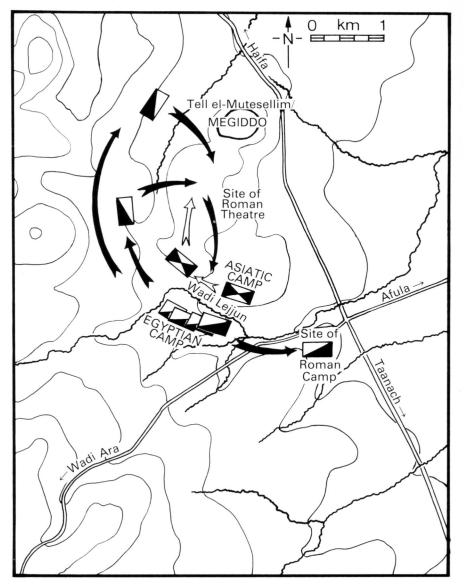

Figure 12 Map illustrating Tuthmosis III's battle at Megiddo. The dark arrows mark Egyptian movements before and during the battle, the white arrows those of the 'Asiatics'. (Andrew Brown; based on the Ordnance Survey 1:20 000 map of Palestine (1942), with permission, Crown copyright reserved)

Egyptian left wing, which threatened both encirclement and a direct assault on the city. The position of the enemy army is described in another inscription of Tuthmosis III, the Jebel Barkal stele, as 'in the Qina Valley *and away from it*, in *a tight spot*' (*ANET*, p. 238), which probably includes a reference to an attempt to extend the defensive line northwards as a counter to the Egyptian manoeuvre.

The Egyptian attack was probably directed against the enemy's right flank, where the approach was easier though still disadvantageous to the Egyptians. Few details of the attack were recorded:

> Thereupon his majesty prevailed over them at the head of his army. Then they saw his majesty prevailing over them, and they fled headlong [to] Megiddo with faces of fear. They abandoned their horses and their chariots of gold and silver, so that someone might draw them (up) into this town by *hoisting* on their garments. Now the people had shut this town against them, (but) they [let down] garments to *hoist* them up into this town. (*ANET*, p. 236)

The annalist is critical of the sequel: the Egyptians missed the opportunity to follow up their success with an immediate assault on Megiddo itself, because they were distracted by the booty and prisoners which awaited them in the enemy camp. As a result Tuthmosis had to make preparations for a siege. A moat was dug around the city, a wooden stockade was built, sentries were posted, and the Egyptians waited. It is evidence of the strength of Megiddo's fortifications and its supplies of food and water that it was able to hold out for seven months (as the Jebel Barkal stele tells us) before surrendering. The only archaeological evidence of the defences so far identified with any probability is the 2–3 metre wall of Stratum IX in Area AA, which may still have been in use, but further study of the numerous cuts which Schumacher made through the slopes of the tell, where he found a succession of city walls, may add to this. It is also still unclear how the population secured access to water during the siege, as the protected approaches to water supplies so far excavated are all of a much later date. It is possible that the approach to a water source whose existence is conjectured below (pp. 71–2) for the eleventh-century city was already in use in the fifteenth century.

There are some difficulties in reconciling the accounts of the surrender and subsequent events in the different accounts which have survived, and it seems likely that the Annals refer in part to later measures designed to establish Egyptian control over Palestine. The list of booty, however, must relate to the original battle:

> [List of the booty which his majesty's army carried off from the town of] Megiddo: 340 living prisoners and 83 hands; 2,041 horses, 191 foals, 6 stallions, and . . . colts; 1 chariot worked with gold, with a *body* of gold, belonging to that enemy, [*1*]

fine chariot worked with gold belonging to the Prince of [*Megiddo*] ..., and 892
chariots of his wretched army – total: 924; 1 fine bronze coat of mail belonging to
that enemy, [*1*] fine bronze coat of mail belonging to the Prince of Meg[iddo, and]
200 [*leather*] coats of mail belonging to his wretched army; 502 bows; and 7 poles
of *meru*-wood, worked with silver, of the tent of that enemy. (*ANET*, p. 237)

Other figures most probably refer to provisions gathered from the surrounding country during the siege:

Now the army [of his majesty] carried off [*cattle*] ...: 387 ..., 1,929 cows, 2,000
goats, and 20,500 sheep.... Now the fields were made into arable plots and assigned to inspectors of the palace – life, prosperity, health! – in order to reap their
harvest. List of the harvest which his majesty carried off from the Megiddo acres:
207,300 [+x] sacks of wheat, apart from what was cut as forage by his majesty's
army,... (*ANET*, pp. 237–8)

These figures give some indication of the vast agricultural resources of
Megiddo, based on successful exploitation of both the plain to the east and the
hills behind, and presumably on effective political control over much of the
surrounding region, of which we shall gain further glimpses from the Amarna
correspondence (below, pp. 59–60).

It is surprising, on first consideration, that there is little archaeological evidence of the successful siege of Megiddo by the Egyptians. In most of the
areas excavated there is no evidence of a destruction that can be dated to the
early fifteenth century BC. A possible exception is the area of the *Nordburg* and
*Mittelburg* excavated by Schumacher, which we have suggested were parts of the
royal palace complex. Here there was evidence of destruction in the *Mittelburg*
above the burial-chambers described earlier, probably dating to the fifteenth century, and it would be possible to connect this with the events of the
siege. Tuthmosis III's inscriptions make no reference to any general burning
of Megiddo after its capture – it was, as we shall see, to serve as a faithful ally
of Egypt – but it would not be surprising if the king's palace had been singled
out for burning as a penalty for his leading role in the opposition to Egypt,
which is also evident in the placing of Megiddo second (after Kadesh) in the
list of the cities conquered by Tuthmosis (*ANET*, p. 243).

It was the view of Olga Tufnell and Kathleen Kenyon that after the siege
Megiddo remained unoccupied for nearly a century. That this conclusion,
which they drew from their study of the archaeological evidence, and
especially from the pottery, is incorrect is indicated by two texts from the
fifteenth century which also attest Megiddo's role at that time as an important
vassal of Egypt. One is an Egyptian papyrus, P. Hermitage 1116A, which
gives two almost identical lists of emissaries, mostly from northern Palestine,
who were supplied with provisions. In each case the representative from

Megiddo heads the list, which suggests that he had a position of leadership in these delegations. The emissaries are designated as *maryannu*, a word of Indo-Aryan origin which refers to the Hurrian aristocracy who fought in chariots. Occurrences of this word and Hurrian and Indo-Aryan personal names indicate that in the fifteenth and fourteenth centuries BC an alien ruling class had gained power in many of the cities of southern Syria and Palestine. The other text is a cuneiform letter found at the neighbouring site of Taanach (which is also mentioned in P. Hermitage 1116A) in excavations at the beginning of this century. This letter (Taanach no. 5) was written by an Egyptian official (or king?) called Amenophis to Rewašša, who was probably the king of Taanach, and it instructs him to send a party of charioteers (presumably *maryannu*), some horses, an additional gift and some prisoners to Amenophis at Megiddo by the next day. This must mean that Amenophis himself was already at Megiddo and probably implies that Megiddo was at this time the centre of Egyptian administration in northern Palestine.

The next strata on the tell, Stratum VIII in Areas AA and DD and Stratum VIIA in Area BB, must therefore belong to the fifteenth century, and not the fourteenth century, as Kenyon thought. In these levels the practice of burial within the city, which had been prevalent since the beginning of the Middle Bronze Age, suddenly ceases, and in all the areas there is evidence of new structures on a grander scale than before. The palace in Area AA, first built in the Middle Bronze Age, was enlarged still further and was surrounded by walls two metres thick on all sides (figure 13). In the south it apparently extended beyond the limits of the excavation area. A new large court, 20 metres by 11 metres, lay at its centre, with another smaller court to the south-west. Between the two courts was a small room that was probably used for bathing. The floor was covered with sea-shells set in lime-plaster and at the centre was a shallow basin of basalt, which was connected to a drain. Two similar but smaller shell pavements, one of them built over a drain, were found by Flinders Petrie at the entrances of buildings at Tell el-Ajjul. Something of the wealth of Megiddo at this time can be seen from a hoard of ivory and gold which was found under the floor of one room of this palace. To its east and a little lower down the slope was a large city-gate, the lower courses of which are still visible to the right of the main approach to the summit of the mound. The walls were faced with fine ashlar masonry, which appears at Megiddo for the first time in this period, but behind the facing was a core of rubble and earth. Some of the lower approach, paved with stones and supported by retaining walls was also found. Inside the gate was an open area paved with lime plaster and from it a flight of basalt steps (of which parts of six were found) led up to the level of the palace above. On the other side of these steps was another large building, but most of it was destroyed by the foundations of later structures. Beneath

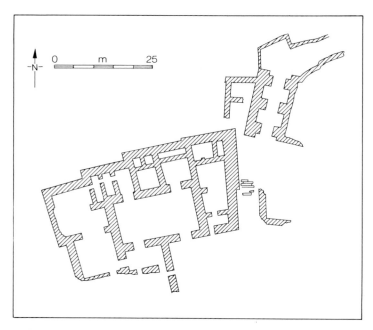

Figure 13   Fortress and city gate of the fifteenth century BC (Stratum VIII). The outer
approach to the city is at upper right. (Andrew Brown; based on *Megiddo
II*, figure 382)

ground level a drainage system carried excess water from the street and the
roofs of the adjacent buildings to the outside of the city.

The excavations in Area DD exposed part of yet another large building of
Stratum VIII about 50 metres to the east of the gate. Again there was a large
court at the centre, 15 metres by 11 metres in this case, with some features
including a small mud-brick platform coated with lime-plaster (an altar?),
which suggest that it may have been part of a shrine. In Area BB the houses to
the south-east of the sacred area continued, with a generally similar plan to
before, but a building with a new, more regular plan and thicker walls (2090)
takes the place of one of the more easterly houses. Temple 2048 belongs, it
seems, to a later stage of Stratum VIIA and will be dealt with in connection
with the Amarna age. Little that is coherent remains to the west of the sacred
area, as here too the foundations of later buildings have disturbed the deposits, but it seems that both the *Nordburg* and the *Mittelburg* were rebuilt after
Tuthmosis III's attack and they may have continued for a time to serve as the
royal palace.

58

## Megiddo in the Amarna period

For developments in the following centuries Area BB offers little clear evidence, and it is chiefly to Areas AA and DD in the north that we must look for clues to the history and character of Megiddo down to its conquest by the Israelites around 1000 BC. In both areas the large buildings described above continue to exist with a slight raising of the floor level, but the palace west of the city gate is more compact and its walls are thinner in Strata VIIB and VIIA. This change appears to correspond approximately to the Amarna period in Egypt, when the rising power of the Hittites and subsequently the religious reforms of Amenophis IV or Akhenaten (1364–47) had led to a weakening of Egyptian power and a consequent loss of influence over affairs in the Levant. We are particularly well informed about Palestinian history at this time through the discovery, from 1887 onwards, of a diplomatic archive at Akhenaten's new capital city of Akhetaten, now (Tell) el-Amarna. The archive comprises over 350 texts written in cuneiform, of which the great majority are letters to the Pharaoh (in certain cases not Akhenaten but his father Amenophis III) from rulers of cities in Palestine and Syria. Some similar texts have been found at Palestinian sites, and at Megiddo a chance find by a shepherd in the 1950s brought to light part of a tablet on which was written a section of the Epic of Gilgamesh in cuneiform. This most likely derives from a scribal school at Megiddo, where apprentices practised the art of writing by copying out standard works of literature. Though brief, the fragment (which corresponds to part of Tablet VII of the late version) shows that the text of the Epic had not yet been fixed in its 'canonical' form. The use of cuneiform in correspondence between Canaanites and Egyptians is a valuable if surprising indication of the way in which Mesopotamian culture, for a time, extended its influence over Canaan, just as we know that it did further north at Ugarit and other Syrian cities.

Eight of the main archive of letters from el-Amarna were sent from Megiddo, most of them by Biridiya, who was apparently the king, or governor, of the city at the time (nos. 242–8, 365: nos. 244–5 are translated in *ANET*, p. 485). His name appears not to be Semitic and he was probably a member of that alien ruling class whose existence is already attested a century earlier, just like many of the other rulers in Palestine during the Amarna period. His letters are full of declarations of loyalty to Egypt: 'To the king my lord and my Sun say: Thus (says) Biridiya, the loyal servant of the king. At the two feet of the king my lord and my Sun seven times and seven times I fall down'. (no. 244.1–8) Megiddo was a place where Yašdata, the pro-Egyptian king of another city could find refuge when he was driven out by an uprising; and when the city of Shunem on the other side of the plain of Esdraelon had been

59

abandoned, it was Biridiya (alone, he claims) who organised a labour-force to cultivate its fields, probably to send the produce to Egypt (nos. 248 and 365).

From several of the letters it is clear that Biridiya had had to contend with hostile forces himself after the withdrawal of an Egyptian force:

> Let the king know that, since the regular troops were withdrawn, Labaya has begun hostilities against me and we cannot shear the sheep(?) or (even) go out of the gate because of Labaya, since he learned about it. And you have (still) not given (us) regular troops. Behold, surely he is determined to capture Megiddo. But may the king hold his city and not let Labaya capture it, after it has been overcome by death and plague and dust ... (no. 244.8–33).

The letter concludes with a renewed appeal for a garrison of a hundred Egyptian troops, to prevent the city from falling into Labaya's hands. Labaya is often mentioned in other letters from el-Amarna as a king or chief from Shechem (40 km south of Megiddo, near the modern town of Nablus), who is for ever intriguing against the rulers of other cities. He appears as the leader of people referred to as SA.GAZ or *ḫapiru*, a group about whose identity there has been much discussion since the Amarna letters were found, because many of their activities resemble closely those of the 'Hebrews' of the Old Testament. It has even been thought that the words *ḫapiru* and 'Hebrew' (*'ibri*) might be related in origin, but this is not at all certain. In the Amarna letters the *ḫapiru* appear as raiders whose forays threatened many cities in Palestine, but they are mentioned in many other texts from as far apart as Egypt and Mesopotamia.

Labaya's attempt to take Megiddo apparently failed, for another letter which is probably from Biridiya (no. 245) tells how he was captured and was about to be sent to Egypt by ship when his supporters bribed the king of Acco to release him. Biridiya made a further attempt to take him alive but he was killed by others before he and Yašdata could arrive. This was not the end of Biridiya's troubles: 'Let the king my lord know, behold two sons of Labaya have paid their silver to the SA.GAZ and to men of K[asi?]-land, who have come against me. So let the king take care of [his land]!' (no. 246. vs 4–11) The activities of Labaya's sons and the SA.GAZ again spread panic throughout Palestine and we do not know what the outcome was.

## A Late Bronze Age Temple

An intriguing possibility arises from the fact that a new temple seems to have been built in the sacred precinct at Megiddo about this time. This is a rectangular building (Temple 2048), three successive phases of which are shown

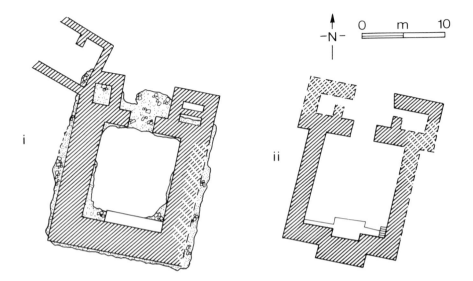

Figure 14  Plan of the two phases of Temple 2048. Broken lines indicate conjectural restorations. In the plan of phase (i) the outline of the underlying 'rubble pavements' is shown as a dotted area. (Andrew Brown; based on *Megiddo II*, figures 401, 403 and 404)

in the American report on the plans of Area BB for Strata VIII, VIIB and VIIA (figure 14). The Stratum VIII stonework is certainly (as the excavators recognised) foundational, so only two real stages of construction need to be distinguished. The single chamber, 11.5 metres by 9.6 metres, was surrounded by massive walls over three metres thick, with two wings, probably towers, flanking the entrance on the north side. Only a single floor level was identified, but rebuilding could be discerned in the raised platform at the inner end and in the main walls, which were reduced in thickness (figure 14). A flight of basalt steps led up to the later and higher platform and the drawings appear to show that it began from a higher floor level than the main one, which may have been overlooked by the excavators.

The period of construction of the temple is a matter of controversy. Two factors have been thought to favour a Middle Bronze Age date: its location and the existence of a very similar structure at Shechem (cf. pp. 48–9). The site which it occupies overlaps the eastern part of the Early Bronze IV temple (4040) which continued in use during the first part of the Middle Bronze Age. Given the general continuity of sacred sites, it is not likely (so it is argued) that a long gap would have elapsed between the abandonment of that temple and the construction of Temple 2048. Moreover, the similar temple at Shechem, which was first discovered in the 1920s and is still (unlike Temple 2048 at Megiddo) visible at that site, has been shown by more recent excavations to have been built in the Middle Bronze Age. Since these two temples form such an unusual group, it is reasonable to suppose that they belong to the same period. Further support for this view is claimed to have been found in an examination of the eastern limits of the excavation area by archaeologists from the Hebrew University of Jerusalem in 1965, but some uncertainties remain in their interpretation of what they found. On the other hand – and this seems to be a decisive argument – Kenyon observed that the broken walls and floors around the site of Temple 2048 marked on the plans of Strata IX, VIII, VIIB and even VIIA indicate the demolition of parts of buildings from these periods in order to make room for its construction. Apparently a deep trench was dug into these levels and a series of 'rubble pavements' were laid in it to stabilise the ground beneath the heavy foundations of the temple. Its origin must be later than the initial phase of Stratum VIIA and perhaps therefore, on the dating followed here, falls in the fourteenth century BC. The finds reported from the temple and contemporary deposits nearby raise no difficulty for this view and could be as late as the twelfth century, when the temple went out of use, along with other major buildings in the city. Neither of the main arguments for a Middle Bronze Age date is conclusive. While, as we have already seen (p. 49), the area probably did retain its sacred character in the period between the abandonment of Temple 4040 and the building of Temple 2048, most of the evidence relating to this interval was dug out in preparation for the laying down of the 'rubble pavements'. It is only this constructional work which has made it appear as if there was a long break in the continuity of sacred buildings in this area. As for the resemblance to the temple at Shechem, it should first be noted that this temple continued to exist throughout the Late Bronze Age and was in fact rebuilt after a period of abandonment c.1450 BC. Evidently temples of this type remained in vogue. But why should such an unusual type of temple (for Palestine) suddenly have been built at Megiddo in the fourteenth century? The Amarna letters offer one possible explanation. As we have seen, it is clear from the latest letters that were sent to Akhenaten by Biridiya of Megiddo that he was under great pressure from the sons of Labaya at Shechem and had to plead with the Egyptians for support. If, as seems very likely, such support was not forthcoming or was to no avail and Megiddo came under the domination of Shechem, this would provide a setting in which the construction at Megiddo of a smaller version of the great 'fortress-temple' at Shechem would be quite understandable.

The finds from Temple 2048 clearly reflect its cultic function and make some interesting contributions to our knowledge of Canaanite religion. They

(a)                                (b)

Plate 10  Cultic objects from Temple 2048: (a) bronze figurine of deity overlaid with gold (b) clay liver model for divination (*Megiddo II*, plate 238.30 and 255.1)

include, in addition to a range of jugs, bowls, flasks and lamps, several figurines of both bronze and clay. One of the bronze figurines, which was found in the destruction debris of the temple, had been coated with gold (plate 10(a)): It represents a seated figure with an oval crown, holding in its left hand a 'standard' which is embossed with a four-pointed star. There is little doubt that this figurine and the others represent the deity worshipped in the temple, but there is no clear evidence of his identity. The seated or enthroned position probably indicates that he was conceived of as a king, which would (in the light of our other knowledge of Canaanite religion) suggest an identification with either El or Baal. Another figurine, of clay, belongs to a well-known type of female figurine which is connected in some way with fertility rituals. Two clay models of animal livers found near the temple point to the practice of extispicy, the examination of the entrails of sacrificed animals, particularly the liver, to predict the future (Plate 10(b)). This is best known in the Near East from texts found in Mesopotamia, and the fact that a similar liver model from Hazor is inscribed with cuneiform omens shows that the Canaanite priests were familiar with this kind of Mesopotamian 'science'. Other objects probably used in the cult are crescent pendants in both gold and bronze and four small bronze cymbals. A collection of bronze objects buried beneath the floor may be a foundation-offering.

# The ivory palace

It is Stratum VIIB which represents the Amarna period (or immediately post-Amarna) buildings in Areas AA and DD: as Kenyon pointed out, the correlation between the different areas made by the American excavators was not always accurate. The palace in Area AA was of more modest proportions now, but two features of it are of particular interest. One is a room in the north-west corner which could be approached both from the main courtyard and from some smaller rooms to the south: it has a flight of steps leading to a platform along one wall. The excavators suggested that it might be a household shrine, but in the absence of any distinctive small finds this is not certain. Another possibility is that it was an audience-chamber. The other interesting feature is a large painted 'clay shrine' (now exhibited in the Oriental Institute Museum in Chicago). It is not fully preserved, but was probably about a metre high and 40 cm square at the top. There is a frieze around its upper part, decorated with trees, wavy lines, crosses and squares, and one side shows four wild animals. Several of the designs are found on ordinary pottery of this period and it is possible that it is simply a piece of domestic furniture, without any cultic associations.

Among other small finds two seals, a cylinder seal of the Mitannian 'popular' type and a stamp seal with Hittite hieroglyphs on it, reflect the influence of the two major powers to the north of Palestine. These were found in Area CC in the south of the city, in an area from which three more cylinder seals were recorded in Stratum VIIA. A gold ring, found in a tomb on the lower slopes, bears an inscription in the proto-Canaanite script of the fourteenth or thirteenth century, which seems to read ḥg lnštrby, perhaps 'A ring(?) belonging to Nišitrabiya'. Finally we should note the growing popularity of amulets in this and the following strata. Small figurines of deities, animals, symbols such as the sacred eye and even parts of the human body had long been in use in Egypt as a protection against evil, but at Megiddo at least they are rare before the final century of the Late Bronze Age.

The palace of Stratum VIIB evidently suffered a catastrophe (perhaps an earthquake), as both the courtyard and the room with the shell pavement (which had continued in use) were filled with debris from fallen walls, and the floor level of Stratum VIIA seems to have been a metre and a half higher. This destruction can be dated towards the end of the thirteenth century on the basis of the pottery. The evidence from Area DD to the east of the gate is very similar, and it is possible that the raising of the floor in Temple 2048 in Area BB took place at the same time. In all three areas the large buildings were rebuilt on essentially the same plan, which suggests that there was no break in occupation. The walls of the courtyard of the palace in Area AA were painted and traces of blue, green, red, yellow, black and white paint survived, but it was not possible for the excavators to make out any design. One important change in the layout of the palace was the addition of an underground cellar block of three rooms, one behind the other, built into earlier debris on the west side. This proved to be a treasure-house, and it contained a collection of ivories (many of them now on exhibition in Chicago) which give a rare insight into the artistic and technical skills of the age, as well as casting some light on more mundane practices such as board games. Fortunately one piece, a pen-case that had belonged to an Egyptian royal official, is inscribed with the name of Pharaoh Rameses III (c.1184–53), which provides an upper limit both for the destruction of Stratum VIIA and for the completion of this collection: neither can be dated much before the middle of the twelfth century BC. Not that all the pieces need be as late as this, for such a collection could well be put together over a period of generations, and one of the pieces certainly seems to be at least a century older.

The ivories (382 pieces in all, though some are very small) represent several different kinds of workmanship. Some bear incised designs, while others are carved in high or low relief and yet others are in openwork in combination with one or both of these techniques. They can be divided into four main categories according to the use to which they were originally put. A large group were intended for the ancient equivalent (whatever it was) of a lady's dressing-table. There are single and double combs, several kinds of bowls, probably for cosmetics, mirror handles, flasks, fan handles or fly swatters, and a square casket beautifully carved form a single piece of ivory (plate 11). All these were decorated, some with simple geometrical designs, others with scenes drawn from nature or mythology. Another major group consisted of plaques which were probably mounted on furniture as a means of decoration. The dowel holes and tenons by which they were fixed are often clearly visible. Some of these depict scenes from battle or everyday life as well as myth and nature. Five more pieces which have hieroglyphic inscriptions are probably to be assigned to this group. One of the inscriptions reads: '(Meat offerings?) for the *ka* of the singer of Ptah-South-of-his-Wall, Lord of "Life-of-the-two-lands", Great prince of Ashkelon, Kerker'. Two others mention the same person, who must have served the Egyptian god Ptah in one of his temples, probably at Ashkelon on the coast of southern Palestine. The inscriptions incidentally provide explicit evidence of the worship of an Egyptian deity in Canaan. A third category comprises boards and pieces for some well-known ancient games, the 'Game of Twenty Squares' and the 'Game of Fifty-Eight Holes' (or 'Dogs and Jackals') (plate 12). They seem to have been 'race games' and lots or dice of some kind would have been required, though none were reported at Megiddo by the excavators (unless this is the significance of some seventy

Plate 11 Ivory casket from Stratum VIIA hoard (G. Loud, *Megiddo Ivories*, no. 1a)

sheep *astragali* found in a tomb of Middle Bronze Age date). Finally there is a unique piece, a plaque only 10 cm square which shows a meeting between two kings in Hittite style standing under winged sun-discs and supported by the Hittite pantheon and, at the bottom, four bulls. R. D. Barnett has suggested that it is a record of a political treaty, either between the Hittites and another kingdom or between a Hittite king and his successor. It was customary for the gods to be cited as the witnesses of such treaties, so their presence is readily understandable. Historians of Near Eastern art have investigated the places of origin of the ivories and have concluded that examples of Mycenaean Greek and Syrian workmanship are present as well as purely Canaanite pieces.

With the ivories were many other precious objects, including pieces of gold jewellery and necklaces. Most probably the whole hoard represented the disposable wealth of the owner of the palace rather than objects that were still in regular use. This would account not only for their presence in an underground chamber and their mixed character but also for the fact that pieces of the same ivory carving were sometimes quite widely separated in the deposit.

Much of the pottery assigned to this phase has recently been shown (by Professor Trude Dothan) to belong to the preceding period, but several new types can be discerned and decoration with groups of horizontal and vertical bands of paint begins to appear, as well as some early Philistine wares. Professor

66

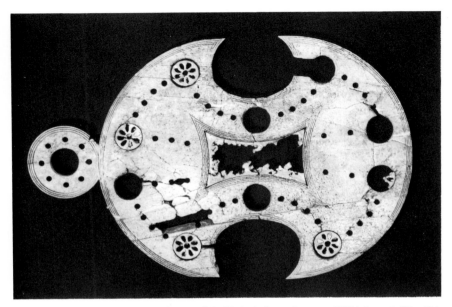

Plate 12 Ivory board for the 'Game of 58 Holes', from Stratum VIIA hoard (*Megiddo Ivories*, no. 221)

Dothan has published a number of Philistine sherds from the American excavations which were omitted from the publication. These fit well with the date suggested by the Rameses III cartouche and point to the growing influence of the Philistines at Megiddo at this time.

## The Early Iron Age City: Canaanite, Philistine or Israelite?

Stratum VIIA marks the end of a long period of continuity in the town-plan of Megiddo. The palace in Area AA (where there is some evidence of burning in the northern rooms), the large building in Area DD and Temple 2048 were all abandoned and replaced by the small, poorly-built dwellings of Stratum VIB. The fact that so much treasure was left where it was in the palace vaults also implies that the previous rulers were driven out at this time. A date a little later than the time of Rameses III for this crisis may be required by an inscribed bronze statue-base found buried in debris of Stratum VIIB (plate 13). The hieroglyphic inscriptions indicate that it carried a statue of Rameses VI (*c*.1142–35). It was certainly not *in situ* where it was found, and it is most

Plate 13  Inscribed bronze statue base of Ramesses VI found buried in Stratum VIIB
(*Megiddo II*, figure 374)

likely that it was buried during or at the end of the period represented by Stratum VIIA. It must imply that even in the reign of Rameses VI Egyptian control was still effective at Megiddo, just as it was at the same time at Beth-shean, but the treatment meted out to it equally points to the likelihood of a repudiation of that control in his reign or soon afterwards.

It is not possible to say with any certainty who was responsible for the attack soon after 1150 BC which brought about such a dramatic break in the history of Megiddo. The neighbouring city of Taanach was apparently destroyed about the same time and not reoccupied for over a century, so it was no isolated occurrence. Some understanding of the possible causes of the upheaval can be gained from a brief review of the general history of Palestine in the thirteenth and twelfth centuries, as it may be reconstructed by a critical examination of the textual evidence which is available. Egyptian control over Palestine was re-established after the Amarna interlude by Sethos I (*c.*1304–1290) and remained firm through most of the thirteenth century, although there is evidence of both Rameses II (*c.* 1290–1224) and Merneptah (*c.* 1224–04) having to campaign against city-states who rejected their suzerainty. Rameses III still had a 'frontier in Djahi (Syria-Palestine)' and collected 'dues of the land of Djahi', and the Harris Papyrus lists among his benefactions to the gods the building of a temple for Amon in 'Canaan', where non-Egyptians came to bring their tribute (*ANET*, pp. 260, 262). After his reign, however, the texts cease to report either royal expeditions to Palestine or administrative activity there. Beth-shean apparently remained loyal to Egypt, and so did Megiddo for a short time, but these were now the exceptions rather than the rule. The idea that the fall of Megiddo VIIA may have been connected in some way with the decline of Egyptian power gains some support from this wider view.

The same texts of Merneptah and Rameses III which speak of their continuing hold on their Asiatic dependencies mention newcomers, whose growing power in the twelfth and eleventh centuries BC is also attested in the Bible. Merneptah's victory stele, dated in the fifth year of his reign (*c*.1220), makes the first (and so far only) reference to Israel in an Egyptian text (*ANET*, p. 378). It is likely that the 'Exodus group' of Israelites had arrived in Palestine shortly before this and that they gradually united with other groups of a similar character who had entered the land separately. Passages in the Old Testament such as Judges 1 (cf. Joshua 17:11–18) and 2 Samuel 2:8–9 show, contrary to the impression given by the book of Joshua, that at first the Israelite tribes were for the most part confined to the hill-country and Transjordan and that the chariot-forces of the lowland cities, which will have included Megiddo, were seen as a particular threat (Joshua 17:16). Archaeological evidence of new settlements from this period in Galilee, the central hills and the Negev can plausibly be associated with the Israelites. There is little indication in the Old Testament of open conflict between the Israelites and the Canaanite city-states from the initial period of settlement until the reign of David, but one major battle (deriving according to the text from a period of Canaanite domination of the tribes) is described in Judges 4 and 5, and it took place in the immediate vicinity of Megiddo (cf. 5:19 – 'in Taanach by the waters of Megiddo'). On the most likely reading of the text it must have taken place while Taanach was still occupied, which in the light of the archaeological evidence now seems to mean before the last quarter of the eleventh century. The biblical accounts, which consist of a victory song as well as a prose account, report the result as a crushing victory for the Israelites, so that it is certainly conceivable that it was followed up by a successful attack on the adjacent cities of Taanach and Megiddo. Nevertheless, the absence of any celebration of such an attack in the biblical accounts must make this hypothesis very unlikely. It has been argued, as we shall see in a moment, that the ensuing occupation at Megiddo (Stratum VIB) is an Israelite settlement, but even if it were it would not necessarily follow that it was the Israelites who destroyed the earlier city of Stratum VIIA: they might simply have occupied the ruined site after it had been destroyed by others who had no wish to settle there.

The other new group is referred to in the Bible as the Philistines (e.g. Joshua 13:2–3, Judges 3:3), but the Egyptian inscriptions show that the Philistines (*prst*) were only one of a number of groups which were known collectively to the Egyptians as 'Peoples of the Sea'. Some of these groups are already mentioned in the inscriptions of Merneptah, but it was in the eighth year of Rameses III's reign that they made a determined assault, by land and sea, on the Nile Delta (*ANET*, pp. 262–3). The Egyptians were able to repel this attack and carried the campaign into 'Djahi', but the Sea Peoples were eventually able to settle on the coast of Palestine. According to the Harris Papyrus this was done with the approval of the Pharaoh: 'I settled them in strongholds, bound in my name. Their military classes were as numerous as hundred-thousands. I assigned portions for them all with clothing and provisions from the treasuries and granaries every year.' (*ANET*, p. 262). Two of the cities occupied by the Philistines were long-standing centres of Egyptian influence in Canaan: Ashkelon and Gaza. Further to the north, at Dor, another group of the Sea Peoples, the Tjeker, had become dominant by the middle of the eleventh century, when they figure in the story of Wen-Amun (*ANET*, p. 26). Archaeological evidence also shows that the limits of Sea Peoples' settlements were not limited to the Pentapolis mentioned in the Bible, but extended as far north as Tell Qasileh and Aphek (Ras el-Ain) on the banks of the river Yarkon. The biblical references to the Philistines give no indication of their dependence on the Egyptians (except possibly in Genesis 10:13–14), and it was probably short-lived, in view of the Egyptians' loss of control over Palestine generally soon after the death of Rameses III. It is possible to identify a period of enlargement of Philistine domination towards the end of the twelfth century (as suggested by Professor Dothan) and the destruction of Megiddo VIIA and Taanach could easily be attributed to this, though if so the Philistines apparently did not take advantage of their success and colonise these sites, as Taanach was left unoccupied and very little Philistine pottery is reported from the following level (VIB) at Megiddo. At the present time much must remain obscure about the extent and pace of Philistine expansion in the lowland areas: the archaeological evidence is not fully clear, while the biblical sources are concerned with (generally later) conflicts between the Philistines and the Israelites but, understandably, not at all with the expansion of the former at the expense of the Canaanite city-states.

It is time to return to the description and interpretation of the archaeological evidence at Megiddo itself. The period of reoccupation (Stratum VIB) was clearly defined only in Areas AA and DD in the north of the mound and even here there are no complete building plans. The site of the earlier palace was occupied by much smaller buildings, although they are well-built for their size. There are no signs of any fortifications or a gate from this period. In several buildings rows of pillars are used instead of solid walls between some rooms: this is a characteristic found in later levels at Megiddo and at many other sites from the early Iron Age on. Stone-lined pits and ovens are also present in considerable numbers, confirming the domestic character of the buildings. In Areas BB and CC Strata VIB and VIA were not distinguished, but because of the distinctive type of mudbricks used in Stratum VIA (see below) it is sometimes possible to identify buildings belonging to a different town-plan as relics of the earlier phase. Some contemporary structures seem to have been found by Schumacher above the *Nordburg* (his 'Stratum III Upper'), including cisterns and basins linked by channels for separating out pure olive-oil. The pottery and small finds ascribed to this phase are meagre and undistinguished for the most part, even when one allows for the likelihood that some objects from the undivided Stratum VI in Areas BB and CC belong to Stratum VIB. There is an increasing tendency to decorate jugs and jars with groups of narrow horizontal bands and a few Philistine pieces occur, though not as many as in the following phase (VIA). Everything suggests that Stratum VIB represents a relatively brief period of occupation.

It was followed by a period in which a large, palatial building once again stood in Area AA, with a small city gate to the east of it and a continuous block of slighter rooms extending to the west. In Area DD too there are remains of some larger buildings once again. In both these cases the major buildings and parts of others are constructed out of an unusual kind of reddish, partially baked bricks on stone foundations. These building materials help to identify buildings of the same period in Areas BB and CC. In the south-east of the latter area it is also possible to recognise the structure excavated by Schumacher and called by him the 'Southern Gate' (squares S 10–11) and its plan can be completed from Schumacher's drawings. It was a rectangular structure 17 metres by 10 metres with walls a metre thick and openings in the south-east and north-west (the latter with an impressive stone threshold 2.50 metres wide). Another distinctive feature of the architecture of this period is the use of wooden posts to partition off sections of some houses, particularly in the south of the city. The spaces between them are very narrow, which suggests that they may have supported a screen of some kind.

There are signs that by this time, if not earlier, Megiddo had been provided with a protected access to a dependable water-supply. We are not referring here to the systems in the south-west of the mound discovered by the Chicago expedition. These were dated by the excavators to the twelfth century, but they are in fact later and they will be described in their proper place in the next chapter. We are concerned here with evidence of an earlier system which was recognised by R. S. Lamon in a depression near the city gate in the north, which can still be seen, and it can be supplemented by reference to the great depth (some eight metres) of 'sterile earth' encountered a little to the west in the southern part of Loud's test-trench. This is a filling of some kind and it could belong to a once open approach to a water channel deep under the tell. Overlying buildings of Stratum VB show that we are dealing with a hollow that was excavated not later than Stratum VIA, and it could be much older (cf. p. 55). Canaanite water-systems are already known at Gibeon and possibly at Jerusalem ('Warren's Shaft') and Gezer, and further excavations in this area could show that Megiddo also had one.

Large quantities of pottery were found in the rooms of the palace, as well as a variety of bronze objects and, just outside it on the west, three bundles of silver pieces wrapped in cloth. The silver is a mixture of earrings, pendants and such like with flat pieces, some of them bearing incised decoration, which have been cut from larger objects, perhaps cups or dishes. The excavators suggest that the silver had been prepared for melting down in a workshop; another possibility is that it represents a payment of some kind made to the ruler of Megiddo or a merchant. The most impressive metalwork came from the southern part of the city, where an unprecedented quantity of bronze jugs, bowls and strainers were found in a single locus (1739) along with the more common axeheads and spearheads. It is interesting that Schumacher also found a quantity of bronze objects in almost the same place. Evidently he penetrated the destruction debris of Stratum VI (A) – which is what he referred to as the *Brandschicht* or 'burnt layer' – and in it he reports finding a double axe-head, two hoes, a javelin, four iron knifeblades and five bronze stands. The latter had a tripod support (in one case four legs) mounted on a ring base, and stood about 35 cm high. A flat bronze dish was mounted on top and in some cases this had clearly been used for burning something. The vertical part of one stand had been cast in the form of a naked female figure playing a double flute and decorative motifs are also evident elsewhere. The pottery of this period shows considerable Philistine influence, perhaps enough to establish that Megiddo had now (c.1100 bc) become a Philistine outpost. One Philistine jug is particularly noteworthy (figure 15), because the main frieze of its decoration depicts a scene of animals surrounding a lyre-player, a most unusual case of the portrayal of the human form by a Philistine painter. Similar scenes are known on seals from southeastern Turkey of a slightly earlier date, and it has been suggested that they are early representations of the Orpheus legend. Another possibility, proposed by B. Mazar, is that the animals are the subject of the musician's song. The presence of a White-Painted Cypriote bowl points to the beginnings of a recovery of wider trading relations.

In Area CC eight large storage jars (*pithoi*) of a type which is characteristic of this period ('collared-rim storage jars') were found, and Schumacher found two more a little to the east. These have often been regarded as distinctively Israelite in origin, because they are generally found at sites in the hill-country, where (as we have seen) the Israelite tribes first settled. Chiefly on the basis of

Figure 15  Frieze of Philistine jug found in Stratum VIA (*Megiddo II*, plate 76)

this evidence Y. Aharoni (following a suggestion first made, but later with-drawn, by W. F. Albright) has argued that Megiddo Stratum VI was an Israel-ite settlement. There are difficulties with this argument. First, the presence of these storage jars may be due to trade rather than the local population of Megiddo. Second, these jars seem rather insignificant alongside a great mass of pottery of a character quite different from what is usually found at Israelite sites. We have mentioned the Philistine influence, and note needs also to be taken of the increasing popularity of decoration with groups of horizontal bands of paint. Thirdly, it is by no means certain that this type of jar is distinc-tively Israelite, as examples have been found in areas well outside the limits of Israelite settlement, for example in Transjordan and in the Plains of Esdraelon and Acco. It is unfortunately not clear whether the loci in which the jars were found derive from Stratum VIB or VIA, and it is on that distinction that any reconstruction of the history of Megiddo in this period must rest.

As we have seen, the destruction of the city of Stratum VIIA was followed by a short-lived settlement of a village character, which in its turn was replaced by the flourishing city of Stratum VIA, with its palace and foreign contacts and highly developed metal industry. The settlement of Stratum VIB could conceivably be Israelite, though this cannot be proved. On the other hand, it is most improbable that this can be said of Stratum VIA, which has a much stronger claim to be regarded as Philistine. A telling argument is that Stratum VIA ends with a massive destruction, which was noted both by Schu-macher and by more recent excavators. It is highly likely that this reflects cam-paigns of David against the Philistines, about which we are only imperfectly informed in the Bible (2 Samuel 5:17–25, 8:1). Megiddo was certainly in Israelite hands by the time of Solomon (1 Kings 4:12, 9:15). We are nowhere told how or when it was captured, but since it evidently did not form part of the territory claimed by the Israelites at the time of Saul's death (2 Samuel 2:8–9: Jezreel here as elsewhere refers only to the city of that name, not the whole region), it can only have been conquered under David.

If Megiddo VIB was a short-lived Israelite settlement at the site, we may conjecture that it was a group from the tribe of Issachar that occupied it, for it was to Issachar that Megiddo and the other cities of the Jezreel plain and valley were originally assigned, according to Joshua 17:11. It appears from Genesis 49:14–15 that Issachar was forced to accept subjection to a Canaanite (or was it a Philistine?) overlord, a situation which might easily be reflected in the transition from Stratum VIB to VIA at Megiddo. The majority of the tribe seems subsequently to have been restricted to a more easterly region (Joshua 19:17–23—cf. 1 Kings 4:17), so that when the need still to conquer Megiddo is mentioned in Judges 1:27 (a document of the time of David or later) it is the powerful tribe of Manasseh which is said to be responsible for it (cf. Joshua 17:11).

*Further reading*

The primary evidence for these periods is found in *Megiddo II*, *Megiddo Tombs* and *Megiddo Ivories*; and in *Tell el-Mutesellim I*, pp. 11–23, 37–74, and *Tell el-Mutesellim II*, pp. 1–25 (the 'fortresses'). For fuller details of these volumes see p. 24 above. Further analysis is provided in Shipton, *Notes . . .*, and K M. Kenyon, 'The Middle and Late Bronze Age Strata at Megiddo', *Levant* 1 (1969), 25–60. For general accounts of the archaeology and history of Palestine in the second millennium see K. M. Kenyon, *Archaeology in the Holy Land*, 4th ed., pp. 148–232, and *The Cambridge Ancient History*, 3rd ed., II/1, pp. 77–116 and 526–56; and various authors in *The Cambridge Ancient History*, 3rd ed., II/2, pp. 98–116 (Amarna letters), 307–37, 359–78, 507–60.

For the MB I period there is now an excellent detailed study by P. Gerstenblith, *The Levant at the Beginning of the Middle Bronze Age*, ASOR Dissertation Series, 5 (Winona Lake, 1983), which has an extensive bibliography. She is able on pp. 23–8 to distinguish three or four MB I phases at Megiddo by a re-examination of the stratigraphy in Area BB and on p. 114 she discusses the date of the city wall ascribed here to MB I. She regards the date as not settled, but appears to incline towards a date early in MB II. Caution is certainly necessary, but I do not think that there are in fact any conclusive arguments to support a MB II date.

On particular topics see: O. Tufnell, 'The Middle Bronze Age Scarab-Seals from burials on the mound at Megiddo', *Levant* 5 (1973), 69–82; J. A. Wilson, 'The Egyptian Middle Kingdom at Megiddo', *AJSL* 58 (1941), 227–36 (the Thuthotep inscriptions); J. N. Tubb, 'The MB IIA Period in Palestine: Its Relationship with Syria and its Origin', *Levant* 15 (1983), 49–62; C. Epstein, *Palestinian Bichrome Ware* (Leiden, 1966); R. Amiran, *Ancient Pottery of the Holy Land* (Jerusalem, 1969); M. Artzy *et al.*, 'Imported and Local Bichrome Ware in Megiddo', *Levant* 10 (1978), 99–111 (on chemical analysis: cf. *Journal of the American Oriental Society* 93 (1973), 446–61); H. H. Nelson, *The Battle of Megiddo* (Chicago, 1913); W. F. Albright, 'A prince of Taanach in the Fifteenth Century BC', *BASOR* 94 (1944), 12–27; J. A. Knudtzon, *Die El-Amarna-Tafeln* (Leipzig, 1907–15); A. F. Rainey, *El-Amarna Tablets 359–379* (Neukirchen-Vluyn, 1970); Dunayevsky and Kempinski, *ZDPV* 89 (1973), 180–4 (Temple 2048); R. D. Barnett, *Ancient Ivories in the Middle East*, Qedem Monographs, 14 (Jerusalem, 1982), pp. 25–8; H. J. R. Murray, *History of Board Games other than Chess* (Oxford, 1952), pp. 12–23; T. Dothan, *The Philistines and their Material Culture* (Newhaven, London and Jerusalem, 1982), pp. 70–80; Y. Aharoni, 'New Aspects of the Israelite Occupation in the North', in J. A. Sanders (ed.), *Near Eastern Archaeology in the Twentieth Century*, Festschrift for Nelson Glueck (Garden City, 1970), pp. 254–67. I have dealt more fully with the twelfth and eleventh century remains in an article 'Megiddo in the Period of the Judges', which is to be published in a forthcoming issue of *Oudtestamentische Studien*.

*Note on terminology and chronology*

Disagreement over the nomenclature for the different archaeological periods continues to be a problem for the Middle Bronze Age. Those (like the Chicago expedition) who refer to the period described in the preceding chapter as 'Middle Bronze I' use the term 'Middle Bronze II' (subdivided into IIA and IIB–C) to cover what we, following Kenyon and Dever, have here called MB I and MB II. For the dates of Egyptian kings the chronology given in the revised edition of *The Cambridge Ancient History* is used up to the beginning of the New Kingdom, but for the Eighteenth and following dynasties it is about twelve years too high. We here follow the chronology worked out by E. Hornung, *Untersuchungen zur Chronologie und Geschichte des Neuen Reiches* (Wiesbaden, 1964), while recognising that a further lowering of the dates may soon be required: see M. L. Bierbrier, *The Late New Kingdom in Egypt* (Warminster, 1975).

# 5

# Israelite Megiddo

## Resettlement under David

Archaeological evidence of the reign of David has so far proved difficult to identify with any certainty, but some biblical passages suggest that in Jerusalem at least he did initiate some building, as is certainly to be expected (2 Samuel 5:9, 11; 1 Chronicles 11:8, 14:1). If our reasoning in the previous chapter is correct, Stratum VB at Megiddo will represent the reconstruction of the city under David, consequent upon its falling into Israelite hands. The remains of this stratum have been found in all the excavated areas, but they are most coherent in Area B (=CC) in the south of the mound. Even here much is unclear owing to the removal of stones by the builders of the following period and the deep foundations of their monumental buildings. Several blocks of rooms can be identified with a common orientation, but there is no clear street plan. Generally only the stone foundations of walls survive, but in a few places the mudbricks remain in place on top. The floors were of beaten earth, except for a few areas with rubble paving, which were probably open to the sky. Lime-plaster floors are notably absent in this phase. The overall impression is one of careful but unpretentious architecture. Only in Area DD was anything that might be a public building traced and the remains were both too few and too intertwined with those of the next phase for any deductions about its use to be possible. There is no evidence of any city wall, but it does seem likely that the approach road and the small gate in Area AA, which were attributed by the excavators to Stratum VA, belong here. This follows from the discussion of later structures in this area (below, pp. 90–2) and is also supported by the fact that a room (2161) contemporary with the approach road rests directly upon debris of Stratum VIA. This gate is too small to have served any defensive purpose and it may simply have marked the entrance to the city, where according to the Bible it was customary for legal and commercial transactions to be executed. Given our incomplete knowledge of the city plan at this stage, it is also possible that the houses on the perimeter of the mound formed a defensive ring, as was the case (in part) in the ensuing period at Megiddo and also at some other early Israelite settlements, for example in the Negev.

Plate 14 Bronze figurine of fighting god from the time of David (Stratum VB) (*Megiddo II*, plate 239.31)

Plate 15 'Manger' from the ninth-century 'stables' (E. P. Todd)

Only a few finds of this level were clearly identified in the reports, but they can be supplemented with those attributed indiscriminately to Stratum V in Area A, because it is now clear (cf. below, pp. 86–7) that Stratum VA is represented in this area by the higher level which the excavators called Stratum IVB (palace 1723, its courtyard and the adjacent building 1482). The structures and the finds which underlie this must belong to Stratum VB. A large quantity of domestic pottery was found here and most of it is of the typical tenth-century type, with an irregularly hand-burnished red wash overlaid on the clay. A few pieces of Cypriote 'Black-on-Red' ware are present. The other finds show that bronze was still the most widely used metal, though iron was coming to take its place where sharpness was important, as in knives and arrowheads (cf. 2 Samuel 12:31). Amulets of various kinds continue to appear, and probably to be included among them is a type of bone pendant, sometimes plain but often decorated with rows of circles with dots in the centre, which is characteristic of the Israelite monarchy period. Even more telling is a bronze figurine of a fighting god, which fully maintains the Canaan–ite tradition (plate 14). It is quite possible that the population of Megiddo remained mainly Canaanite in composition even after the city was incorporated into David's kingdom. The Canaanites did not simply disappear overnight.

There is no evidence at this stage of Megiddo having occupied a position of any political importance in the kingdom. Indeed it was probably the case that throughout the land the organisation of the population and the planning of their towns differed little under David from what it had been under Saul and the judges, despite the incorporation of areas which had hitherto resisted Israelite efforts at expansion. The narratives of 2 Samuel certainly point to the establishment of a court in Jerusalem (8:16–18; 20:23–6) and some preliminary attempts to organise the kingdom (2 Samuel 24), but it is clear from them that the tribal structure of the people had remained intact (15:2, 10; 19:9; 20:14; 24:2) and that, as has often been noticed, the major division between Israel in the north and Judah in the south was not overcome. 1 Chronicles 27:16–22 gives a list of the 'princes' or 'leaders' of the different tribes in the time of David (cf. 1 Chr 28:1) and this may reflect something of the constitutional arrangements of the time, even if (as seems likely) the lists in this chapter are predominantly later fictions.

## Solomonic Megiddo: the American excavations

The excavation of the upper layers on the mound has made it clear that this was only a temporary eclipse of Megiddo's importance, as it was quickly built up, and then rebuilt, with strong fortifications and massive public buildings of various kinds. Unfortunately our account of this cannot be straightforward, as the relationships between the buildings of Strata VA, IVB and IV and the placing of the occasions of their construction within the history of Israel during the tenth and ninth centuries BC have been controversial questions ever since their discovery. At the present time it is no longer possible to speak, as it was ten or fifteen years ago, of a consensus on these topics. The next few pages will therefore be devoted to a review of this protracted and continuing discussion. Not only is this the clearest way to present the finds and the different points of view; it will also serve as a useful illustration of how and why archaeologists may disagree in their interpretation of the same data. At the end an attempt will be made to give an assessment of the arguments used and to present a defensible account of the architectural history of Megiddo in the early monarchy.

Our starting-point must be the buildings ascribed by the American excavators to their Strata VA, IVB and IV (figure 16). *Stratum VA* was best attested in Area AA, where in addition to the small gate and approach already mentioned there was a row of houses parallel to the edge of the tell. Their outer walls had been destroyed by the deep foundations of the city wall of Stratum IV. In a corner of the courtyard in front of one of these buildings (locus 2081) a quantity of small limestone altars was found, with offering stands, pottery of various types and other objects. Two upright stones in an entrance nearby were interpreted as *maṣṣebot* or pillars associated with Canaanite worship. Only parts of buildings from this period were identified in Areas BB and DD, but we should add to them the structures published without further qualification as Stratum V in Area C (in the east of the mound), as in several cases they overlie buildings known to belong to Stratum VB. Here too there is an almost continuous line of houses parallel to the edge of the mound, with floors paved either with rubble or with lime-plaster. One long narrow building (Building 10) seems likely to have been a storehouse: it contained a lot of pottery, and a layer of ash and the burnt grain in some of the jars are evidence of destruction at the end of this period. Close by was a building with eight upright stones, in two rows, which were thought at first to be possibly *maṣṣebot*, and the discovery of more small altars and pieces of pottery shrines nearby

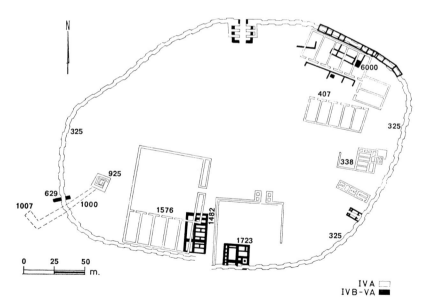

Figure 16  Plan of the major structures in Strata VA/IVB and IVA. The long building south of Building 338 (i.e. Building 10, cf. above) also belongs to Stratum VA–IVB, as Yadin recognises elsewhere. (From Y. Yadin, *Hazor* (Schweich Lectures), figure 39)

seemed to support a cultic interpretation of the building. In fact, as is now clear, it is one type of the ubiquitous 'four-room house'. The pottery of this stratum again included many pieces with hand-burnishing over a dark red wash, but also Cypriote pottery of both the 'Black-on-Red' and 'Bichrome II' types. Other finds included two iron axes, amulets (with four 'sacred eyes' among them), a necklace, a silver earring, a small game board and numerous female clay figurines.

The excavators found it necessary to subdivide their Stratum IV in the south of the mound, for two reasons. The city wall of this period was built over the rear of a palatial building which they also ascribed to Stratum IV; and the 'Southern Stables' overlay the northern and western rooms of another building of the same stratum. The two lower buildings, which were also linked by a lime-plaster pavement and their common orientation, were therefore referred to as *Stratum IVB*. The 'palace' (Building 1723) was a rectangular structure 23 metres by 21.5 metres, with an extension at the north-east corner which was initially thought to be a foundation for a porch. Only foundation-courses remained *in situ* but these showed that the walls were 1.25–1.50 metres thick and sufficient to carry a second storey. A study of the layout of the building by Professor D. Ussishkin has noted some similarities to palaces of the so-called *bit-ḥilani* type known in northern Syria and also to the description of Solomon's palace in Jerusalem (1 Kings 7:6–12). It is possible to identify provisionally an entrance on the north side, an open court within the building, a throne- or audience-room and two staircases leading to the upper floor. The palace stood in a large courtyard about 60 metres square, which was paved with lime-plaster and had a small gatehouse in the north-east corner of its enclosure wall (which Schumacher had already found and erroneously called a 'palace'). The adjacent building (1482) was rectangular and originally measured *c*.35 metres by 15 metres. There was nothing to indicate its function clearly, but it may have served some administrative purpose.

In its main, later, phase the city of *Stratum IV* was surrounded by a solid city wall at the top of the slope, *c*.3.60 meters thick. About half of this could still be traced during the excavation. Its plan was unusual, as it was constructed in sections about 6 metres long which were alternately set in or out by about 50 cm (plate 16). The surviving portions of the wall are entirely built of stone, some of it finely-hewn stone that must have been taken from older monumental buildings.

With the possible exception of two stones, only the foundations of the city gate ascribed by the excavators to Stratum IV were found *in situ*, but even they make plain its massive plan and fine masonry technique. It was a rectangular structure 15 metres by 12 metres, with solid foundations for two towers at the

Plate 16  Section of the city wall of Stratum IV, showing 'offsets' and 'insets' (*Megiddo I*, figure 39)

outer end and three matching chambers on each side of the roadway behind them (figure 17). The roadway itself was *c*.4.25 metres wide. A door-socket was found in place by the inner end of the western tower and it was presumably matched on the east side, for the mounting of double doors. There was an outer gate some 30 metres down the roadway and the space between the two gates was strongly defended, forming a kind of bastion. A hall that opened on to the western side of this area may have been a guardroom, with its roof providing a useful defensive position. One curious feature which the excavators observed but could not explain was that the main gate and the wall of the outer court were not bonded into the city wall: Lamon describes this as 'from a structural point of view inexcusable'. Two additional features of the gate complex were a stone-built drain which passed under the city wall just west of the main gate and a (possibly subterranean) stairway that led straight down the steep slope from just outside the outer gate. The latter, which seemed to be a secondary addition, was originally thought to be a short cut for pedestrians entering or leaving the city, but Yadin has now shown that it provided access to a pool or water channel connected with the spring north of the tell.

Parts of a few buildings were identified inside the wall in Area AA, with one exception of small proportions. In the south only a few walls remained of the building which replaced Palace 1723, and the adjacent 'administrative building' (1482) continued in use at a much reduced size. The major structure in this part of the city was now the so-called 'Southern Stables' (Building 1576), which consisted of a large court about 55 metres square with two rooms on its east and a row of long, narrow rooms on its southern side. These latter rooms clearly fell into five units of three rooms each. In each unit the outer two rooms were floored with rubble while the central room was floored with lime-plaster and, while the walls dividing each unit from the next were of the normal type, each central room was divided from its flanking rooms only by a row of stone pillars, with spaces of about a metre between them. Stone 'mangers' had stood between these pillars, or at least between some of them. The horses, it was supposed, stood in the side aisles and the central room provided access to them for the stable staff. Holes in the pillars were thought to be for tethering the horses. The courtyard was floored with lime-plaster and laid on a filling of earth to level the ground surface, and great ingenuity was employed to keep this filling stable and to drain it. In the centre was a brick-built 'cistern', perhaps for watering the horses.

Similar buildings were discovered in the north-east of the city in Area C and are referred to as the 'Northern Stables' (plate 17). The later excavations in Areas BB and DD added to our knowledge of them and a missing corner in the south-west was found on Schumacher's plan of the *Nordburg*. Instead of using a filling to level the ground in this area, as in the south, the foundations were cut down into earlier levels, so that in places they are close to the floors of Stratum VIIA and no evidence of Stratum VI survives. Some of the levelling seems already to have been carried out prior to the construction of a similar building in Stratum V(A?), as walls on a slightly different line, but of the same general plan, were found just below the floor level of Stratum IV. Blocks of 'stable units' were situated around three sides of a slightly skew rectangle, five units on the north, two on the east and five again on the south. The space between the three blocks was not open but was occupied by a large building of which parts were discovered at three different points in the excavation. It is clearly of a different type from the 'stable units', yet to judge from its position it must have been connected with them. It may perhaps have been a barracks or a supply depot.

To the south-east lay another, smaller building of the same type and a small 'palace' (Building 338) which was set in its own enclosed courtyard. Part of

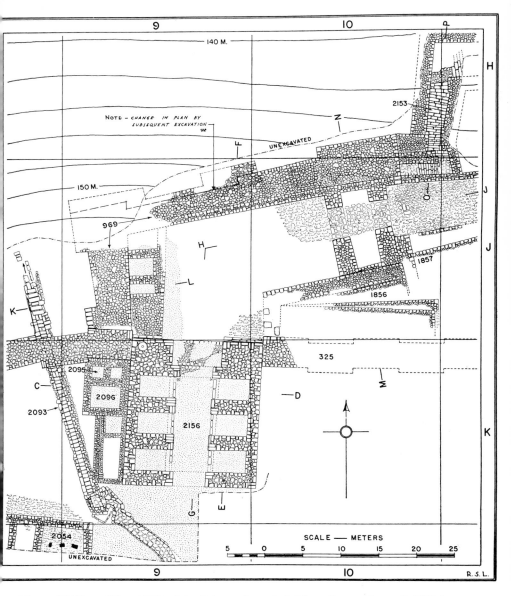

Figure 17  Plan of Gate 2156 of the Solomonic period. The adjacent city wall (325) is probably of later construction. (*Megiddo II*, figure 105)

83

Plate 17   Unit of the 'Northern Stables' of the ninth century (*Megiddo I*, figure 50)

this had been excavated by Schumacher beneath what he called 'the Astarte temple'. The three surviving courses of masonry formed a podium filled with debris from earlier levels, approached by steps along the northern side. The upper courses and the floors of the living accommodation had been destroyed, so that there can be no certainty about the location of doorways, but the plan suggests a tower in the east, from which an excellent view could be had of the plain below. Burnt remnants of the superstructure indicate that it was made of timber (as analysis showed, of cedar) and mudbrick, but it is too much to claim, as the excavators did, that they point clearly to the pattern of 'three rows of hewn stone and a row of cedar beams' known from the description of the courts of Solomon's temple (1 Kings 6:36, 7:12). The masonry was particularly fine, with ashlar piers at the corners and at intervals along the outer walls. The excavators gave special attention to the function of this building, which had been claimed as a temple by H. G. May in one of the earlier publications of the expedition. They were able to show that the arguments put forward in favour of a cultic function proved nothing and concluded that it was most likely 'a private residence of an important personage', such as the commander of the east of the city.

Given the above grouping of the buildings into three successive phases, it was thought that several factors could be used to date them. It was believed in the mid-1930s that hand-burnishing of pottery gave way to wheel-burnishing c.1000 BC, so the distinctive pottery of Stratum V placed it entirely before that date. An approximate date for the beginning of that stratum (i.e. of VB) c.1050 BC was deduced from the twelfth century date then thought likely for Stratum VI and the belief that a period of abandonment had elapsed after its destruction. This conclusion seemed to be confirmed by the ascription of the very similar Stratum II at Tell el-Ful (supposedly Gibeah) to the reign of Saul. P.L.O. Guy had already in 1931 proposed to date Stratum IV to Solomon's reign, partly because of references to the building of chariot-cities and Megiddo in particular in the biblical account of Solomon's reign, but also because of archaeological parallels to the 'stables', the pottery in them, some 'aegis of Bastet' amulets which he thought were from the time of Sheshonq I (whose reign overlapped with Solomon's) and the non-Palestinian character of the masonry of Stratum IV. He also held that Megiddo would have been an ideal centre for the trade in horses and chariots carried on by Solomon, and that the wood and stone construction of Building 338 reflected a technique used in Solomonic Jerusalem. The final report added that a fragment of a stele of Sheshonq I, found on the mound (figure 18), demanded that Megiddo be occupied c.930 BC and since (it was thought) Stratum V ended about 1000 BC Stratum IV must already have been in existence then. Further, the association in Stratum IV of hand-burnished pottery with wheel-burnished pottery seemed to fit the tenth century better than any later period, as the Harvard excavations at Samaria were thought to have shown that already in the ninth century hand-burnished pottery had gone out of use. It should be noted that the excavators' dating of Stratum IV was not based merely upon a desire to find 'Solomon's Stables' at Megiddo, although this correlation did play a part in it. Granted a Solomonic date for the main phase of Stratum IV, it followed that the closely similar Stratum IVB represented a small outpost on the tell built either under David or early in Solomon's reign.

## Solomonic Megiddo: debate and new discoveries

When these conclusions were reviewed by other archaeologists, two major lines of criticism soon emerged. J. W. Crowfoot, who as Director of the British School of Archaeology in Jerusalem had been excavating at Samaria in the middle years of the American work at Megiddo, was strongly critical of the arguments used to associate Stratum IV with Solomon. He had himself found very similar architecture at Samaria which dated from the ninth century, and

Figure 18  Fragment of a stele of Sheshonq I found at Megiddo (R. S. Lamon and G. M. Shipton, *Megiddo I*, figure 70)

Figure 19  Seals of (a) Shema and (b) Asaph (Andrew Brown; based on C. Watzinger, *Tell el-Mutesellim II*, figures 61 and 62)

he proposed that the major buildings at Megiddo were likewise built, not by Solomon, but by the house of Omri. He pointed out that the Bible did not actually say that Megiddo was one of Solomon's chariot-cities, but distinguished it from them (cf. 1 Kings 9:15, 19), so that the 'stables' of Stratum IV were unlikely to be Solomonic. Moreover, the hand-burnished pottery of Stratum V could not be limited to a date before 1000 BC, since he had found it in ninth-century levels at Samaria. Later Kathleen Kenyon, in the final report on the pottery from Samaria, was to go further and to claim that the pottery in the constructional fill under the 'Southern Stables' and Building 338 included types known from the mid-ninth century levels at Samaria, so that these buildings could not have been constructed before that date.

Meanwhile two American archaeologists, W. F. Albright and G. E. Wright, had also been busy studying the excavators' reports, and they made the important contribution of showing that Stratum IVB in the south of the city and Stratum VA('V') in the north and east were not successive phases but parts of one and the same level, dating from the time of Solomon. But in other respects they did not in the end dissent very much from the excavators' conclusions about the period under consideration; in fact they added further arguments to support the view that the gate of Stratum IV was Solomonic, including its resemblance to a gate described in Ezekiel's vision of the restored temple in Jerusalem (Ezekiel 40:5–16) which, they supposed, was modelled on a gate in the Solomonic temple.

A more drastic re-evaluation of the whole problem was, however, soon to follow. In 1957 Professor Yigael Yadin discovered in his excavations at Hazor a city gate of the Solomonic period with a plan and dimensions almost identical with those of the gate of Stratum IV at Megiddo. As if this were not enough, he went on to identify one half of a similar gate in a plan from the report of R.A.S. Macalister on his excavations at Gezer fifty years previously. Macalister had referred to this structure as part of a Maccabean palace, but Yadin's hunch proved to be correct when, in 1968 and 1969, new excavations at Gezer, by then under the direction of W. G. Dever, uncovered the other half of the gate and confirmed its tenth-century date of construction. The similarity of plan not only added weight to the arguments for a Solomonic date for the Megiddo gate: it corresponded beautifully to the conjunction of these three strategic sites in the account of Solomon's building works: 'the forced labour which King Solomon levied to build the house of the Lord and his own house and the Millo and the wall of Jerusalem and *Hazor and Megiddo and Gezer*' (1 Kings 9:15).

Yadin had, however, noticed a fly in the ointment, or what he took to be one. While the Solomonic gates at Hazor and Gezer were linked to casemate city walls the gate at Megiddo was linked (it seemed) to the solid 'offsets-and-insets' wall. Being suspicious of such irregularity – for why should the engineers who had in other respects proceeded in such remarkably similar ways depart from their pattern at Megiddo? – Yadin went to Megiddo with a small team of assistants in January 1960 to see whether a casemate wall perhaps existed there too. His task was not easy, for the whole mound had been excavated down to Stratum IV in the 1930s and in many places deeper still. But he found an area to the east of the city gate where the solid wall of Stratum IV was still standing and, even before excavations began, he was able to observe beneath the foundations of the solid wall, a straight wall which proved to be the outer wall of a rectangular fortress *c*.28 metres by 21 metres (Fortress 6000), which was built of ashlar masonry. In due course excavation showed that while this building was earlier than the solid walls (and the 'Northern Stables') it was later than both Strata VIA and VB. In other words it clearly belonged to the composite stratum VA/IVB identified by Albright and Wright, and this was confirmed by some pottery found in one of the rooms. Yadin also ascribed to this stratum a large building to the south, of which he traced the northern wall. This looks very like the outline of the central building of the 'Northern Stables' of Stratum IV (above, p. 82), and a final decision about its stratum must await the full publication of Yadin's excavations.

To the east and west of the fortress Yadin found the casemate wall that he was looking for, nicely sandwiched between the solid wall above and structures of Strata VIA and VB below. To the east the casemates were recognised to be less substantial than at Hazor, but to the west they were strongly built and the line could be traced a little further on the excavators' plan of Area DD (Stratum VB/VA). Unfortunately the earlier excavations of Schumacher and the Americans had made it impossible to follow this line to the city gate itself, but Yadin thought that there was now sufficient evidence to show that at Megiddo too the Solomonic gate had been associated with a casemate wall, as at Hazor and Gezer. More was to follow. Yadin, it seems, could not believe that Solomon dismantled the city of Stratum VA/IVB, as he must have done if he were the builder of the main part of Stratum IV; moreover, the pattern of Hazor (not to speak of Samaria) suggested that a further period of royal building was to be assumed under Omri and Ahab. His chronology of the buildings at Megiddo therefore became:

| | |
|---|---|
| David | Stratum VB |
| Solomon | Stratum VA/IVB, with Fortress 6000, the casemate wall and city gate 2156 |
| (attack of Sheshonq I) | |
| Jeroboam I | 'Stratum IVA1': the solid wall, with reuse of city gate 2156 |
| Omri-Ahab | 'Stratum IVA2': 'Northern and Southern Stables', solid wall, city gate 500 (formerly ascribed to Stratum III) |

Yadin's theory thus envisages two periods of use for Gate 2156, and he believed that they could be correlated with two different roadways, the one (normally attributed to a lower gate of Stratum VA, and here taken to belong to Stratum VB) at the foot of the surviving gate structure, which was therefore wholly above ground level in this phase and had no foundations, and the other level with its top, so that the surviving masonry then came to form the foundations for a superstructure that has completely (or almost completely) disappeared.

In essentials this is also the view accepted by Kenyon in 1971 in the light of Yadin's excavations and arguments, though the evidence from Samaria led her to insist that it was only shortly before 850 BC that the main part of Stratum IV was constructed, and no place was left for an initial rebuilding under Jeroboam. The agreement of these two eminent authorities in Palestinian archaeology – and in America the leading archaeologists also quickly indicated their support – justified one in speaking of a consensus about the architectural history of Megiddo under the early Hebrew monarchy. But it was to be a short-lived or rather, as I suspect, an interrupted consensus. The first blow was struck by Yohanan Aharoni, a former colleague of Yadin in the excavations at Hazor who in due course went his own way and founded the Institute of Archaeology at Tel Aviv University. In a sharply critical article published in 1972 he contested several of Yadin's claims. He emphasised that the solid wall was built against Gate 2156 and could not be separated from it, and that the excavators had found no evidence of a casemate wall in the vicinity of the gate. He also questioned the idea put forward by Yadin that the surviving portions of Gate 2156 had originally stood above ground, rather than being from the outset foundational, since the stones had shown no signs of weathering when they were first excavated and a gate without foundations was inconceivable. As for Yadin's excavations, Aharoni denied on the basis of his own visit to the site that a casemate wall had been found, explaining the 'western casemates' as part of a courtyard associated with Fortress 6000 and the 'eastern casemates' as the outer rooms of houses forming a ring around the mound, as had been found elsewhere in Stratum VA. There was no casemate wall, therefore, at Megiddo and no reason to depart significantly from the stratigraphy and dating proposed by the excavators. Aharoni believed that Stratum VA contained Fortress 6000 and Palace 1723 as well as its own small gate and the ciruit of private houses, and that it had been built by David. To Stratum IVB he attributed the solid wall, Gate 2156 and the 'stables', and he asserted that this had been built by Solomon, perhaps after the destruction of the Davidic city in an Egyptian invasion which he thought might have extended further to the north than Gezer (1 Kings 9:16).

The most recent assessment of the evidence is that of Ussishkin. A careful and very useful review of previous interpretations and of the archaeological evidence from all parts of the city leads him to agree with Yadin and Kenyon that Stratum VA/IVB (with Fortress 6000, Palace 1723, the circuit of private houses and fortifications 'which were probably of the casemate wall type') was built by Solomon and destroyed by Sheshonq I in the fifth year of Rehoboam of Judah (1 Kings 14:25–6), while the main part of Stratum IV ('IVA', including the solid wall and the 'stables') is later. The known facts of Solomon's building at Megiddo and Sheshonq's attack (on the latter see further p. 96) point to these conclusions, whereas Aharoni's theory has to presuppose in addition building activity by David and an earlier Egyptian attack, neither of which is historically attested in relation to Megiddo. The weakness of the Yadin–Kenyon view and the main impulse to Aharoni's chronology, Ussishkin believes, comes from the assumption that Gate 2156 is Solomonic and this, he argues, is a mistaken assumption. His argument is founded on the impression that this gate and the solid wall form an architectural unity and on the absence of any casemate wall (or room for one) adjoining the gate. From this it follows that the gate is contemporary with the solid wall and, since the latter belongs to the post-Sheshonq I reconstruction of Megiddo (Stratum IVA), the gate must do so too and cannot have been built under Solomon. There is no problem in this, since there are similar gates not only in Solomonic levels at Hazor and Gezer but also in a later level at Lachish (Stratum IV) and outside Israelite territory at Ashdod.

## Evaluation of the arguments

It is time to offer some comments on this discussion which may point the way forward to a clearer picture. First, it seems that Aharoni was correct to question Yadin's idea that the 'lower roadway' was once used in conjunction with Gate 2156. The lime-plaster actually extended underneath the eastern tower of that gate, and must therefore represent a street level belonging to an earlier stage of construction, as can be seen from a comparison of the published plans. It is true, as Y. Shiloh has shown, that the excavators themselves were initially inclined to Yadin's theory, but as the work proceeded they found themselves compelled by new evidence to give it up. There is only one roadway associated with the gate, the one which is level with the top of the surviving walls, which are therefore foundational. Secondly, it is possible that Aharoni was right to question Yadin's interpretation of the rooms adjacent to Fortress 6000 as a casemate wall, particularly those in the east. Large parts of the city of Stratum VA/IVB may have been protected only by a continuous line of houses around the edge of the mound, as is known to have been the case in the western quarter at Beersheba and at several other sites.

Thirdly, on the other hand, these criticisms do not affect Yadin's main contention and in general the chronology advocated by him and by Kenyon, with Stratum VA/IVB being Solomonic and Stratum IV(A) being from the ninth century (or the end of the tenth century, after Sheshonq I's invasion), is preferable to that of Aharoni (which is close to that of the excavators and of Albright and Wright). In addition to the argument of Ussishkin to this effect, this view is the only one which is compatible with the pottery evidence from the filling under the 'Southern Stables' and Building 338. As Kenyon showed, this corresponds to Samaria Period III in the mid-ninth century. The validity of this argument is not affected by a separate controversy over the date of the pottery recorded as belonging to Samaria Periods I and II. Fourthly, the identical plan and measurements of Gate 2156 and the Solomonic gate at Hazor (Stratum X), together with the very close similarity of the Solomonic gate at Gezer, make it almost certain that the Megiddo gate is from the period of Solomon too. Were it not for its apparent connection to a ninth-century city wall, there would be no hesitation in accepting that view. So is that connection as secure as it looks? Attention has often been drawn to the fact that the wall and the gate are not bonded into one another. It may be true, as Ussishkin has pointed out, that such bonding in is not essential at the level of foundations. But the lack of it at least permits the conclusion that the two structures were not built at the same time. Furthermore, there is the fact that the solid wall was bonded into the gate ascribed to Stratum III and as a result it was built up not only against but over the abandoned foundation of Gate 2156. This can be seen from a comparison of the plans and arises inevitably from the fact that the city wall continued along the front of the gate of Stratum III. It is also evident from the way in which the discovery of Gate 2156 is described in Loud's unpublished excavation diary (in the extracts which follow 'the gate' means the gate of Stratum III and the 'earlier structure' and the 'heavy walls' are what turned out to be Gate 2156):

(Wednesday Jan. 22 [1936])
A still earlier structure – which is partly under the city wall – has been incorporated as part of the eastern outer pier of the gate. The nature of the earlier structure is not yet clear, but its heavy masonry would suggest fortifications and it seems quite likely that it is an earlier gate. It is definitely under the eastern extension of the city wall but seems vaguely connected with the western extension of what has been considered the same city wall . . .

(Saturday Jan. 25)
The floor of room 504 ['503' in the published report] of the gate was removed, and the heavy, well built walls of some very large structure were revealed. The walls all plunge under the gate – one emerges to the south (this was exposed some weeks ago), another continues east under the stone floor of the gate street, and a third extends northward under the outer western pier of the gate and appears to join (and be contemporary with) the western part of the city wall. Presumably this heavy structure is a part of the one found under the eastern part of the gate – but to the east the heavy earlier walls also underlie the only visible remains of the city wall.

One feature that might seem to conflict with the view that the city wall was built after Gate 2156 is the outer gate and its associated courtyard. It has sometimes been said that the way in which different walls abut against one another implies the following order of construction: first the main gate (2156), then the solid city wall, then the outer gate and its courtyard. If this is correct, then the whole complex, gates and wall, must have been built within a very short period, as the roadway passing through the inner gate corresponds to that which passes through the outer gate. However, on the most detailed plan a gap is shown between the city wall and the wall of the outer courtyard. The most plausible explanation of this gap is that it is due to the cutting back of the courtyard wall to make room for the foundation of the city wall; that is, the construction of the city wall was subsequent to the completion of the gate complex.

Once it is established that the solid city wall is (or can be) later than Gate 2156, there is no difficulty in following the lead of the other arguments and dating the wall to the ninth century and the gate to the Solomonic period. The problem of the fortifications which adjoined Gate 2156 still remains, of course, and it is only possible to suggest what they may have been. This is because the foundations of the solid city wall were laid so deep that in many places they rested on the ruins of Stratum VIA and so whatever existed along this line in Strata VB and VA/IVB was destroyed by the builders of this wall. Only speculation is possible. There may have been a casemate wall, against which the VA/IVB houses were built, which was dismantled by the builders of the solid wall; or these houses themselves, perhaps with a strengthened outer wall, may have formed the defensive line. We shall probably never know, because the builders of the solid wall removed all the evidence. It follows that the consensus established after Yadin's excavations was in most respects soundly based and that the studies of Aharoni and Ussishkin serve to refine it rather than, as they thought, to overthrow it. There is, however, no reason to think that Gate 2156 continued in use after Sheshonq I's attack: when Megiddo was rebuilt, probably in the second quarter of the ninth century, the new gate (500), which was originally attributed only to Stratum III, provided access to the city.

## Water-systems and 'stables'

Yadin's work has one further contribution to make to our picture of the tenth- and ninth-century cities. The American expedition had discovered two protected approaches to a spring in a cave on the south-west of the tell, a stone-built 'gallery' passing beneath the solid city wall (Locus 629) and a vertical shaft linked to a horizontal tunnel dug through the solid rock (Loci 925 and 1000). The latter in particular is a most impressive piece of engineering (plate 18) and the excavators were able to reconstruct in detail how the ancient workmen must have set about their task. Their conclusion was that both systems had been constructed in the twelfth century BC (which is when they dated Stratum VI), when Canaanite Megiddo was under Egyptian control. This date was based on the discovery of pottery characteristic of Stratum VI in the cave by the spring and on the belief that the solid city wall, which passed over the gallery, was built under Solomon. Yadin's examination of the remains of Gallery 629 showed that its masonry included ashlars dressed in exactly the style of the Solomonic buildings and, more important, that it cut through structures of Strata VB and VIA. Taken together with the fact that it was clearly earlier than the city wall of Stratum IV(A), this provided excellent stratigraphical proof that the gallery approach to the spring in the cave formed part of the Solomonic city of Stratum VA/IVB. Since there would have been no point in constructing the gallery when the much more effective shaft-and-tunnel system was in existence, it is to be presumed that the latter system is later and it probably belongs to Stratum IV of the ninth century. Such a date receives some confirmation from the fact that a somewhat similar system to this was found in excavations at Hazor, where there was clear stratigraphical evidence for a ninth-century date; it would also provide a convenient explanation of the origin of the debris used for the filling under the adjacent 'Southern Stables' and their courtyard.

The function of these latter buildings and their counterparts in the north of the city constitutes one final issue which requires consideration before we are in a position to conclude with an overall account of Megiddo's role in the early Israelite monarchy. Professor J. B. Pritchard pointed out that the description of them as stables at the outset depended heavily on the belief that they were built by Solomon and on the biblical passages referring to his 'chariot-cities'. In the light of Yadin's arguments for dating these buildings with the rest of Stratum IV to the ninth century, which he accepts, Pritchard went on to ask whether the archaeological evidence is sufficient by itself to validate the description of them as stables, and he concluded that it is not. He claimed that there was no evidence for the use of stables for horses in the ancient Near East, that the similar buildings at Hazor and Tell es-Saidiyeh were probably not stables and that the so-called tethering-posts, mangers and water-tank could not have been used in the ways suggested. Moreover, the plan of the buildings was unsuited to use as stables, since a horse at the inner end could be taken out only after all those nearer to the entrance had been removed, and the excavators themselves had acknowledged that the objects (such as harness buckles) which one might expect to find in the vicinity of stables were completely absent. The few finds reported consist mainly of domestic pottery. Pritchard suggested that the buildings were possibly storehouses or barracks. Strong support for the first of these alternatives later came from the excavations at Beersheba, where very similar buildings were found near the city gate, packed

Plate 18 The horizontal tunnel cut through the rock for the ninth-century water-system (G. I. Davies)

with storage jars and other kinds of pottery. Storehouses or magazines of this long narrow plan are widely attested in the cities of the ancient Near East.

Most of these points are well made and it must certainly now be acknowledged that the Iron Age pillared buildings are not all stables. On the other hand, further discussion of the matter has suggested that Pritchard overstated his case in some respects. The existence of stables has been demonstrated at Tell el-Amarna in Egypt, at Ugarit and in a relief of Ashurnasirpal II of Assyria, and references to stables occur in records of Ramesses III of Egypt and in Mesopotamian texts (Akkadian *ma"assu, qabūtu* and *urû*). The 'mangers' at any rate could well be just that. The Megiddo buildings are unique in having 'mangers' and, in the case of the southern block, the large courtyard in front is strongly reminiscent of the enclosure next to the stables in the 'police barracks' at el-Amarna and could have been used as a parade-ground. These factors perhaps justify us in continuing to refer to these complexes as 'stables'. It is possible that the same type of building served different purposes at different places and times.

## Summary: Megiddo as an Israelite Royal City

The remains represented by Strata VA/IVB and IV(A) thus provide evidence of Megiddo's status as a royal city with two distinct phases of existence. In the first phase, which we attribute to Solomon, that status is apparently compatible with the continued presence of a substantial population of ordinary civilians within the walls, as indicated by the houses in the north-west and east of the mound. Large areas previously occupied by domestic dwellings have, however, been taken over for the construction of public buildings, particularly in the south and north-east. It is plausible to connect the palace 1723 and the adjacent 'administrative building' (1482) in the south with the government of Solomon's fifth district (1 Kings 4:12), and Megiddo may have been its chief city. Building 10, among the houses in the south-east, seems to have been a public storehouse. If we are correct in discerning an earlier 'stable block' beneath the later 'Northern Stables' (p. 82), it may be that the public buildings in the north-east of the city, including Fortress 6000, were of a more military character. The fortification of the city is most apparent in the very strongly built gate complex and in the provision of protected access to the water-supply in the south-west (Gallery 629). The association of Megiddo with Hazor and Gezer (1 Kings 9.15) suggests a definite plan on Solomon's part to ensure the security of his kingdom and this may have been directed as much towards maintaining the loyalty of the northern tribes by force as to defence against enemies abroad. If so, the effort was counter-productive, for these very measures were a major provocation to secession after his death (1 Kings 11:27, 12:3–4).

The public buildings at Megiddo exhibit a style of masonry which represents a further refinement of the use of ashlars in the late Canaanite period (Strata VIII–VI). It has commonly been presumed that this development was due to the employment of Phoenician craftsmen by Solomon in his provincial cities as well as in Jerusalem (cf. 1 Kings 5:18), but Y. Shiloh has shown that evidence of such masonry has yet to be found this early in Phoenicia. At present it is rather to be ascribed to the workmanship of native Canaanite and Israelite masons, benefiting perhaps from the increasing availability of superior iron tools (cf. 1 Kings 6:7). The so-called 'proto–Aeolic' (or palmette) capitals also appear to be a local development of a traditional artistic motif, and they make their first appearance in this period. The references to palm-tree motifs in the description of Solomon's buildings in Jerusalem can be compared with them (1 Kings 6:29–35, 7:36). The other noteworthy feature of the remains is the large quantity of ritual vessels. These also seem for the most part to reproduce styles well known from the late Canaanite period and the likelihood that many of the old inhabitants had continued to live in the city makes this fully understandable. The small limestone incense altars, which are paralleled all over the country, particularly in this period, may be an exception and could represent an innovation connected with the opening up of the incense trade with south Arabia by Solomon.

This city was attacked by Pharaoh Sheshonq I near the end of his reign, *c*.925 BC. His invasion is mentioned in the Bible (1 Kings 14:25-6; 2 Chronicles 12:2-9) and dated to the fifth year after Solomon's death, but its full extent and the fact that it included a campaign against the northern kingdom only became apparent with the discovery of Sheshonq's own account of it in the temple of Amon at Karnak (*ANET*, pp. 242-3): the list of conquered cities includes Megiddo along with Taanach, Beth-shean, Mahanaim and possibly Penuel and Tirzah. There is only slight evidence of the burning of the city of Stratum VA/IVB (in Building 10) and the fact that Sheshonq erected a stele there may imply that most of it was left intact. A possible explanation for Sheshonq's campaigns against Judah and Israel might relate them to the internal strife between the two halves of Solomon's kingdom which had split apart only a few years before. Jeroboam I of Israel had been an exile at the Egyptian court (1 Kings 11:40) and he may well have sought his former protector's help in his war with Rehoboam (for which see 1 Kings 15:6). The latter, however, was perhaps able to buy Sheshonq off by handing over the temple treasures (1 Kings 15:26) and to persuade him to direct his army against Jeroboam instead.

Whether Megiddo lay in ruins for a time or briefly continued as before, its wholesale reorganisation in the form which it took in Stratum IV is best attributed to the Omride dynasty. Omri's military origin, the need to secure the new dynasty and the resurgent military power of the northern kingdom make this altogether the most plausible time. If they had not already left, it would have been necessary to displace many of the remaining civilian population, for there is very little evidence of private dwellings in the new layout of the city (and very little room for them). The episode of Naboth's vineyard at nearby Jezreel (1 Kings 21) may not have been unique. Megiddo, like the new capital at Samaria, was at this time a strongly fortified acropolis and most of the ordinary citizens presumably lived on the slopes below, where a number of Iron Age dwellings were identified but not properly published. The solid city wall dates from this period, with the so-called 'Stratum III' gate (Gate 500) in its first phase. The largest structures inside are the northern and southern 'stable complexes', and their interpretation largely determines whether we think of Megiddo at this time as a store-city or, as seems preferable, a military base with a strong chariot force. Even on the latter view other buildings (such as the 'central building' in the 'Northern Stables' and the large building southwest of the city gate) will probably have been used for the storage of provisions and military equipment. The city's ability to withstand a long siege depended not only on its strong walls but on the secure and entirely concealed access to the spring by means of the shaft-and-tunnel system. An additional means of obtaining water to the north of the city, where there was another spring, has been identified in the so-called 'pedestrian access' beyond the outer city gate and possibly it too dates from the ninth century. The obvious candidate among the excavated buildings for the governor of the city's quarters is Building 338 in the east, with its own enclosed courtyard. From here there was an excellent view across the plain below. It seems that this building took over the function previously served by Palace 1723, unless the meagre remains above the latter in fact derive from a building of comparable size and grandeur. The 'administrative building' (1482), though reduced in size, presumably continued to fulfil its earlier role. It will have been to this city that Ahaziah king of Judah fled for refuge after being wounded a few miles to the south-east during Jehu's *coup d'état* c.842 BC (2 Kings 9:27).

It is likely that this city remained in existence until the Assyrian invasions in the latter half of the eighth century brought an end, in two stages, to the independence of the northern kingdom. The completely new layout of the city in Stratum III, in which most of the city reverted to domestic occupation, and the strongly Assyrian character of such larger buildings as there were are most readily explained if they are attributed to a rebuilding after the Assyrian conquest. This conclusion seems inevitable and is now generally accepted, but the excavators' own view that Stratum IV ended c.780 BC once found considerable support, chiefly because of the argument from pottery. It does indeed appear that some of the latest developments found at Samaria are missing from the pottery of Stratum IV at Megiddo, but this need not require a date for the latter before the eighth-century Assyrian invasions. It is clear from the textual evidence (see below) that Megiddo fell into Assyrian hands some twelve years before Samaria and the latest developments in style and technique attested at Samaria could have taken place during that period. The capital may also have been somewhat more abreast of the latest fashions in pottery than the administrative and military centre of Megiddo, so that older styles would continue in use longer at Megiddo than at Samaria.

## Megiddo as an Assyrian provincial capital

Evidence of destruction was provided by wood charcoal and burnt mudbrick in the debris of the 'governor's quarters' (Building 338) and the accumulation of debris in the other buildings. The city presumably fell to Tiglath-Pileser III of Assyria (745–727) in the course of his campaigns in northern Israel in 734 or

733 BC. These are mentioned in texts of Tiglath–Pileser himself (*ANET*, pp. 283–4) and also in the Bible:

> In the days of Pekah king of Israel Tiglath–Pileser king of Assyria came and captured Ijon, Abel-beth-maacah, Janoah, Kedesh, Hazor, Gilead and Galilee, all the land of Naphtali; and he carried the people captive to Assyria. Then Hoshea the son of Elah made a conspiracy against Pekah the son of Remaliah, and struck him down, and slew him, and reigned in his stead, in the twentieth year of Jotham the son of Uzziah. (2 Kings 15:29–30; cf. Isaiah 9:1, Hosea 5:11)

These texts make it clear that Tiglath–Pileser annexed the whole of the northern and eastern parts of Israel, leaving Hoshea as ruler only of Samaria itself and the surrounding hill-country. Many of the population were deported and probably, as happened elsewhere, they were replaced by settlers from other parts of the Assyrian empire (cf. 2 Kings 17:24). It is somewhat strange that Megiddo is not mentioned by name in any of the texts, but neither the account in Tiglath–Pileser's annals (which are in any case fragmentary) nor that of 2 Kings gives a full list of the cities that were captured. Megiddo would probably be included in the general expression 'Galilee'. The name of Megiddo does occur in some later lists of the provinces of the Assyrian Empire, and the city was probably therefore the administrative centre of this province, which is thought to have included Upper and Lower Galilee as well as the plain and valley of Jezreel. The name of one of the provincial governors, Itti-adad-a-ni-nu, has survived, because during his period of office he was the eponym official (*limmu*) for the year 679 BC. This meant that documents such as contracts written during that year were dated by his name, and at least two such documents, from Assur, are extant.

The character of the new city was quite different from that of its predecessor, in several ways, although certain features continued in use, such as the city wall, the gate complex and the shaft-and-tunnel access to the spring (the latter two in a modified form). Most of the city was occupied by houses and only in the north does there seem to have been any concentration of public buildings. The large 'stable' complexes were, with one exception (unit 404) abandoned. A large circular stone-lined pit, which can be seen in the southern part of the mound, evidently served for the storage of grain, as some chaff and grain were found in between the stones of its wall. It was at least seven metres deep and had a diameter of eleven metres at the top, giving a capacity of about 450 cubic metres (*c.*12,800 bushels). Such a quantity of grain could support a population of 1,000 adults comfortably for eight or nine months. The pit has two staircases descending around the inside of the circular wall, a unique arrangement which perhaps provided separate routes for descent and ascent. The rest of the city (figure 20) was laid out according to a 'grid' street plan,

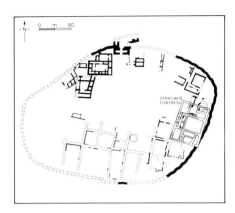

Figure 20  Plan of Strata III and II. The broken lines in the lower part of the plan indicate where the street plan has been reconstructed. (Andrew Brown; based
on *Megiddo I*, figures 71, 72, 89 and 95)

except for the area directly within the city gate, where there was a group of
large 'open-court' buildings. Both these features are foreign to Palestine of the
Israelite period, but well attested in Mesopotamia. The streets could be distinguished by a characteristic deposit of small stones and sherds, even where
house walls were not preserved. The *insulae* or 'blocks' were often divided by
a 'backbone' into houses that faced respectively east and west. The buildings
near the gate have a large courtyard at their centre, with a row of rooms (sometimes two) on each side and well-constructed doorways and drainage-systems.
In one a pillared entrance opens on to the inner quarters. The sloping surface
of the ground beneath them was levelled by artificial fillings and buttress walls
were added to retain them. As a result the floor-levels of these buildings were
raised well above that of the square inside the city gate. We may reasonably
suppose that they were occupied by the governor of the province and his most
senior officials.

One building of this period which attracted much attention in the early
reports on the excavation was the so-called 'Astarte temple'. This was a rectangular room, first discovered by Schumacher and further explored by
Fisher, which was built on top of what turned out to be part of the 'governor's
quarters' (Building 338) of Stratum IV. The original reason for thinking that
it was a shrine seems to have been two pillars built into a central dividing wall,
next to one of which a flat stone formed a shelf or table: these were taken, like
those found elsewhere on the tell, to be *maṣṣebot* or cultic pillars. Schumacher
thought that adjacent walls were part of the same building, but some of them
at least can now be seen to be parts of Building 338, which also explains the

99

'deep foundations' of which Schumacher wrote. The pillars are very similar to those in the 'Northern Stables' nearby and may have been taken from there. In any case there is no reason to see in them or the building any connection with worship: this was already pointed out by Watzinger. Fisher found what he took to be evidence confirming Schumacher's cultic interpretation (and a specific association of the 'temple' with Astarte) a little to the south. This material has already been described (pp. 79–80) and, since it belongs to a much earlier period, it clearly has nothing to do with this structure, which was probably part of an ordinary house.

The finds from this period can best be described after a brief account of Stratum II has been given. There is little change in the layout of the city and for Areas C and D the excavators did not construct a separate plan. In the centre and south of the mound there was more rebuilding, but the street plan remained largely intact and the character of the city was not affected. All this points to substantial continuity and in all probability gradual and piecemeal replacement of old buildings by new ones. A brick floor in square Q8 is reminiscent of an Assyrian building at Tell Jemmeh. The only major difference which the excavators envisaged between Strata III and II was the abandonment of the city wall (and presumably the gate fortifications) in Stratum II and the construction of a fortress in the east of the mound overlooking the plain. Its walls were 2–2.5 metres thick and formed, according to the American expedition's reconstruction, a rectangular enclosure c.75 metres by 50 metres, with northern, southern and western wings around a central courtyard. An eastern wing might be expected, as this was the side most open to attack, and remains of it could perhaps have collapsed down the slope of the tell. The details of the plan are otherwise unclear for lack of evidence. The same difficulty dogs attempts to date the structure securely, and it is not at all certain whether it does belong to Stratum II or to Stratum I of the Persian period. According to the excavators the city was 'subjected to a certain amount of destruction' at the end of Stratum II.

Excavations carried out by A. Eitan in 1974 have added a little to our knowledge of the seventh-century occupation at Megiddo. On the slopes beneath the fortress (squares N–O 16–17) he investigated a building with walls a metre thick and lime-plaster floors, which contained pottery of the late seventh century BC. Because of its size he considered that it was unlikely to be a private house, but its precise function remains uncertain. Its location suggests that even after the abandonment of the major public buildings of Stratum IV there was still insufficient space on the summit to accommodate both the new population and its rulers.

The finds from Strata III and II reflect the changed circumstances of the city and in some cases the arrival of a new population. Several new pottery

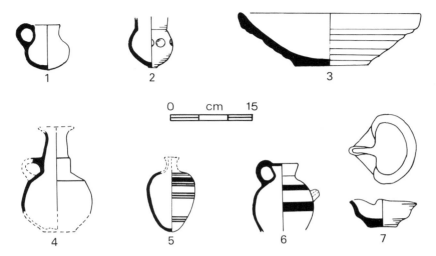

Figure 21  A selection of pottery from the Assyrian period (1, 7 standard late pre-exilic types; 2, 3, 5 Assyrian types; 4, 6 imports from Phoenicia). (Andrew Brown; drawn from *Megiddo I*, plates 1.34, 2.58, 3.78, 9.7, 12, 23.15, 37.7)

types appear, including some paralleled in the Assyrian levels at Tell Jemmeh in southern Palestine and others which appear to derive from Phoenicia to the north. Others represent late pre-exilic types known throughout Palestine (figure 21). It is surprising that hardly any Assyrian 'Palace Ware' has been found at Megiddo, in view of its administrative importance. This is in sharp contrast to other sites in Palestine administered by the Assyrians, such as Samaria, Tell el-Far'ah(N) and Tell Jemmeh, where substantial quantities of this pottery have been found. A large number of metal objects of both iron and bronze and ranging from arrowheads and sickles to jewellery and needles were present, particularly in the southern quarter. The concentration seems heavier than elsewhere in two 'blocks': these may have housed metalworkers. A possible 'smithy' (with iron ore and slag) was identified by Schumacher a little to the east: it seems likely to belong to the Assyrian period. A notable feature is the appearance in these strata of bronze fibulae or clasps of a variety of types. In several cases the pin was of iron, to give added strength and rigidity. Such clasps had been in use in the Near East (as well as the Greek world) for some centuries to fasten clothing, but they are very rare in earlier Israelite strata at Megiddo. This suggests at least a change in fashion and is perhaps also a further indication of a new element in the city population. A similar conclusion may be drawn from a group of small circular stone palettes, with a diameter of 8–10 cm, which begin to appear in Stratum III. They were possibly used for cosmetics. A cylinder seal in Assyrian style points to the new regime, and a jar found in Stratum III has a seal-impression on it which includes the prenomen of Shabako king of Egypt (*c.* 716–702). The latter provides new evidence for the current view that good relations existed between Assyria and Egypt for most of his reign. It was at first taken to point to Egyptian attempts to subvert Assyrian rule in Palestine (cf. 2 Kings 19:9), but the evidence is growing that the respective royal courts maintained trading relations with each other and the Megiddo impression fits well into such a picture.

## Hebrew Seals and other inscriptions

Megiddo has so far produced disappointingly little inscribed material in Hebrew or other alphabetic scripts, compared with other major excavations in Palestine, but what has been found can conveniently be surveyed here. Apart from what may or may not be isolated letters incised on sherds, the corpus at present includes two inscriptions incised on jars, both very short and obscure, and five of the large number of scarab seals from the site. One of the inscribed jars was found by Schumacher in the 'Astarte temple': four letters of the inscription survive, *'bth*, but the meaning is unclear. The other jar inscription consists of the three letters *lyw* and belongs to a large group of inscriptions on jars which all begin with the Hebrew preposition *l*, 'belonging to', followed by a person's name. In this case it is probable that the inscription was not completed rather than, as was once thought, its being a dedication to Yahweh himself. The jar itself was found in a pit ascribed to Stratum II. The use of the Hebrew script in inscriptions from these levels points to the persistence of an Israelite element in the population after the Assyrian invasions, alongside the newcomers.

Seals were widely used in the ancient world to authenticate documents (1 Kings 21:8; Isaiah 29:11) or to stamp official stores or consignments of goods. Large numbers of inscribed seals are known from Palestine and neighbouring countries, but relatively few have come from controlled excavations. Pride of place among those from Megiddo must go to the splendid jasper seal inscribed *lšm' 'bd yrb'm*, 'Belonging to Shema, the servant (or minister) of Jeroboam', around a representation of a roaring lion (figure 19(a)). This was found during Schumacher's excavations in debris above the courtyard of Palace 1723, which was re-used in Stratum IVA. It passed into the private collection of the Sultan in Istanbul, because Palestine was under Turkish rule at the time of its discovery, but its present whereabouts are unknown. A bronze cast of it was made before it left Jerusalem and this can be seen in the Rockefeller Museum there. Both the find-place and the script indicate that 'Jeroboam' is the powerful king of that name who ruled the northern kingdom of Israel in the mid-eighth century BC (c.784/3–753/2), i.e. Jeroboam II. 'bd, which can mean 'slave' or 'servant', is here an honorific title, so that 'minister' is a better translation (compare 2 Kings 22:12 for the title): it refers to a leading figure at the royal court. Megiddo as an important royal city would be a natural place for him to visit or even to live in. Two other seals, of serpentine and lapis lazuli respectively, are probably from about the same time. They have very similar designs, with a winged griffin wearing the double crown of Egypt occupying most of the face of the seal. This design is found on several other north Israelite seals (unlike those from Judah seals from the north nearly all bear a design of some kind) and has clear Phoenician and ultimately Egyptian affinities. One (also in the Rockefeller Museum), which is inscribed ḥmn, 'Haman', shows the Egyptian ankh-sign and a locust in addition, while the other, which belonged to one Asaph (l'sp), has a cartouche in front of the griffin containing meaningless hieroglyphs (figure 19(b)). Like the Samaria ivories these seals show how open the northern kingdom was to the cultural and no doubt religious influence of Phoenicia.

The two other seals are probably not Israelite. One, of lapis lazuli, bears the inscription l'lmr, 'Belonging to Elamar', and an as yet unparalleled design of two uraei and a sphinx. It comes from Stratum II, i.e. the Assyrian period, and the script has been identified as Phoenician of the first half of the seventh century, so that it reinforces the impression given by the pottery of increasing Phoenician influence at that time. The final seal, which is made of glazed faience, remains something of a mystery. It was found during the American excavations on the south-eastern slope of the mound, without an archaeological context, and both its design and its inscription have so far defied interpretation. At the centre there is what has been taken as a very stylised quadruped, while the letters (some of whose forms are Aramaic or Phoenician rather than Israelite) seem to read zbyh/dm(??)q', a sequence which, taken as a whole, makes no sense at present.

## The death of Josiah

The date of the transition from Stratum III to Stratum II cannot be determined precisely and it is probably pointless to try, as with the possible exception of the fortress (if that was built in the Assyrian period) the rebuilding seems to have been piecemeal. The end of Stratum II falls, on the pottery evidence, towards the end of the seventh century, a period of great political movements about which we are comparatively well informed and in which Megiddo once again comes into view in the written sources. From the middle of the seventh century Assyrian control of the empire became progressively weaker, though there is mention of an Assyrian governor in Samaria in 646 BC and a year or two later the Assyrians were able to mount a punitive campaign against Tyre and Acco. Internal struggles, the pressure of marauding tribes and the resurgence of Babylon under a Chaldaean dynasty founded by Nabopolassar hastened this process of decline after the death of Ashurbanipal in 627. The resulting power vacuum in Palestine, on the western edge of the empire, left the way open for both Egypt, under Psammetichus I (664–610) and Judah, under Josiah (640–609), to enlarge their domains. The extent of Josiah's political control can be gauged from the scope of his religious reforms, which according to the more reliable account in 2 Kings 23:19 extended to 'the high places which were in the cities of Samaria' (contrast 2 Chronicles 34:6–7). This would confine his rule to Judah itself and the former Assyrian province of Samaria. A Hebrew ostracon from this period found at Yavneh-yam (Meṣad Ḥashavyahu) has been thought to show that Josiah also controlled part of the coastal plain. The Egyptians, however, held sway over Ashdod, a few miles to the south, and the Phoenician coast. The political allegiance of Megiddo (and its province) at this time remains obscure: some scholars believe that it was in Josiah's hands, others that it must have been held by the Egyptians at least from 616, when they sent a force (presumably overland) to assist the Assyrians in their struggle for survival against the Babylonians and the Medes. The archaeological evidence is not of much help, especially as we cannot be sure that the fortress ascribed to Stratum II was actually built at this time rather than in the Persian period. If it was, it may be significant that those elements in the plan which can be reconstructed with greatest certainty have parallels in the so-called palace of Hophra/Apries (589–70) at Memphis in Egypt.

In 610 the Egyptians again lent help to the dying Assyrian cause, but apparently withdrew without achieving anything. In the following year, as we learn from the Babylonian Chronicle (*ANET*, p. 305), 'a large army from Egypt', now under Neco II (610–595), crossed the Euphrates, probably from their base at Carchemish, and succeeded in entering Haran with Ashur-uballit, the last king of Assyria, only for the latter to be killed in the city. On its way to Syria the Egyptian force passed by Megiddo where, in circumstances that are far from clear, Josiah was killed by them.

> In his days Pharaoh Neco went up to the king of Assyria to the river Euphrates. King Josiah went to meet him; and Pharaoh Neco slew him at Megiddo, when he saw him. And his servants carried him dead in a chariot from Megiddo, and brought him to Jerusalem, and buried him in his own tomb. (2 Kings 23:29–30)

Subsequent tradition (already in the books of Chronicles (2 Chr 35:20–25)) asserted that Josiah confronted Neco in battle but failed to stop his advance, and modern historians who accept the validity of this tradition have sought to explain why Josiah should have taken such a risk to prevent help reaching the beleaguered Assyrians. Was he perhaps in league with the Babylonians? In fact, if taken by itself the account in 2 Kings need not imply that there was a battle at all or any hostile intent on Josiah's part: 'went to meet him' could even mean that Josiah intended to lend support to Neco's expedition. But if so, why was Josiah killed? Perhaps not enough attention has been given to the apparently unnecessary words 'when he saw him'. If they mean anything, they suggest a hasty, perhaps unconsidered, response to Josiah's appearance. Neco may, as has been suggested, have ruthlessly decided that this was a good opportunity to gain control over the whole of Palestine by eliminating his would-be ally. The fact that on his return from Syria he removed the king who had been crowned in place of Josiah and replaced him with a man of his own choice makes such an aim quite likely (cf. 2 Kings 23:31–5). Another possibility is that Neco misinterpreted Josiah's arrival at the strategic battle-field of Megiddo, thought that he was trying to block his way and, without waiting to ask questions, made a pre-emptive strike against Josiah's camp. In any event, what promised to be a new golden age of independence for Judah was suddenly cut short by a foreign army and, even if for nothing else, the Chronicler's account is evidence that this catastrophe was commemorated in a special way (2 Chr 35:25). According to one view, the choice of 'the mountain of Megiddo', Ar-mageddon, as the site for the final battle between the people of God and the Gentile armies in the book of Revelation (16:16) goes back ultimately to the need to avenge the wrong done to this second David:

> Before him there was no king like him, who turned to the Lord with all his heart and with all his soul and with all his might, according to all the laws of Moses; nor did any like him arise after him. (2 Kings 23:25)

(Some have seen a reference to the battle between Josiah and Neco in Herodotus 2.159, which speaks of a battle between 'Syrians' and Neco at 'Magdolus' (Migdal), prior to Neco's capture of Kadytis (Gaza). But this is more likely to be a battle on the outskirts of Egypt itself.)

*Further reading*

The primary evidence for this chapter comes from *Megiddo I, Megiddo Tombs, Megiddo Water-System, Material Remains of the Megiddo Cult, Tell el-Mutesellim I* and the articles by Yadin and Eitan listed on p. 24). For general surveys of the period see K. M. Kenyon, *Archaeology in the Holy Land*, 4th ed., pp. 233–305, and *Royal Cities of the Old Testament* (London, 1971); and Y. Aharoni, *The Archaeology of the Land of Israel*

(London, 1982), pp. 192–279 (his treatment of Megiddo is on pp. 200–11, 222–5: cf. *Journal of Near Eastern Studies* 31 (1972), 302–11).

On particular topics see D. Ussishkin, 'Was the "Solomonic" City Gate at Megiddo built by King Solomon?', *BASOR* 239 (1980), 1–18; Y. Yadin, 'A Rejoinder', *ibid.*, pp. 19–23; Y. Shiloh, 'Solomon's Gate at Megiddo as Recorded by its Excavator, R. Lamon, Chicago', *Levant* 12 (1980), 69–76; G. J. Wightman, 'Megiddo VIA–III: Associated Structures and Chronology', *Levant* 17 (1985), 117–29; J. B. Pritchard, 'The Megiddo Stables: A Reassessment', in J. A. Sanders (ed.), *Near Eastern Archaeology in the Twentieth Century* (Garden City, 1970), pp. 268–76; Y. Yadin, 'The Megiddo Stables', in F. M. Cross *et al.* (ed.), *Magnalia Dei*, G. E. Wright Volume (Garden City, 1976), pp. 249–52 (cf. *Eretz-Israel* 12 (1975), 57–62 (Heb.)); Y. Shiloh, *The Proto-Aeolic Capital and Israelite Ashlar Masonry*, Qedem Monographs, 11 (Jerusalem, 1979); S. Dalley, 'Foreign Chariotry and Cavalry in the Armies of Tiglath-Pileser III and Sargon II', *Iraq* 47(1985), 31–48; L. G. Herr, *The Scripts of Ancient North-West Semitic Seals*, Harvard Semitic Monographs, 18 (Missoula, 1978); R. Hestrin and M. Dayagi-Mendel, *Inscribed Seals* (Jerusalem, 1979); G. Garbini, 'I sigilli del regno di Israele', *Oriens Antiquus* 21 (1982), 163–75; A. Malamat, 'The Twilight of Judah in the Egyptian–Babylonian maelstrom', *Supplement to Vetus Testamentum* 28 (1975), 123–45; R. Nelson, 'Realpolitik in Judah (687–609 BCE)', in W. W. Hallo *et al.* (ed.), *Scripture in Context II* (Winona Lake, 1983), pp. 177–89. An extended refutation of Pritchard's article on the 'stables' was completed some years ago by Professor J. S. Holladay and is scheduled to appear in a volume in honour of S. H. Horn, *The Archaeology of Jordan and Other Studies*, which is to be published in 1986.

*Note on Chronology*

The dates of the kings of Israel and Judah are differently computed by scholars and are given here according to the chronology worked out by K. T. Andersen, 'Die Chronologie der Könige von Israel und Juda', *Studia Theologica* 23 (1969), 67–112, and used in S. Herrmann, *History of Israel* (London, 1975: 2nd English ed., 1981). For other systems and a brief discussion of the problems resulting from the figures given in the Old Testament see J. H. Hayes and J. M. Miller, *Israelite and Judaean History*, pp. 678–83. The dates of Egyptian kings are taken from K. A. Kitchen, *The Third Intermediate Period (1100–650 BC)* (Warminster, 1973).

# 6

# Megiddo under the Persians and Afterwards

Some time in the late seventh century the town of Megiddo seems to have been abandoned. There was some evidence of destruction in the remains of Stratum II. In 605 BC the Babylonian army won a decisive victory over the Egyptians at Carchemish and as a result Syria and Palestine (including Judah, as 2 Kings 24:1 shows) became subject to Babylon. The inhabitants of Megiddo, which may have been an Egyptian base, were probably dispersed by the new rulers. There is at present no clear evidence of any occupation at Megiddo during the period of Babylonian rule (605–539). The American excavators did, it is true, fix the beginning of the occupation represented by Stratum I around 600 BC, because of the presence in it of pottery characteristic of the late seventh or early sixth century along with the later types. But the recent review of the evidence by E. Stern has shown that this is due to confusion in the report between structures which genuinely belong to Stratum I (and have Persian period pottery in them) and those which represent a further stage of reconstruction of the town of the Assyrian period (Strata III–II). Further study of the plans and the lists of finds may clarify the situation and the possibility should be recognised that evidence of Babylonian occupation, which is often difficult to identify at Palestinian sites because of the transitional character of the period from a cultural point of view, may emerge from such research. Much certainly remains to be gleaned from the considerable amount of information about Strata I–III provided in the American report (as well as Schumacher's work), and much more material from other excavations is available now for comparison than was the case when the report was written.

It is not certain whether Megiddo regained its political status as an administrative centre under the Persians or was simply a garrison town. In fact our knowledge of the history of northern Palestine generally during the two centuries of Persian rule (539–332 BC) is extremely slight. The Old Testament sources are interested only in Judah and, to a much lesser degree, in Samaria, while the other literary and epigraphic evidence relates, apart from some references to the northern coastal plain, exclusively to the more southerly districts. The archaeological evidence from Megiddo suggests that in the first phase of the Persian period the southern part of the tell at least was unoccupied by buildings and was used as a burial ground. The excavators found four

107

Plate 19 Cist grave of the Persian period with the covering slabs removed (*Megiddo I*, figure 107)

graves of the 'cist' type there, sandwiched between walls of Stratum II and Stratum I (T.1263 and T.1265 in square O8; T.1276 and T.1277 in square Q8). The dead had been placed in a supine position in rectangular cists about two metres long and 40 cm square in cross-section (plate 19), which were lined with large flat stones and covered with four or five slabs laid across the breadth of the tomb. Graves of this type have also been found at Gezer (the so-called 'Philistine graves'), Ugarit, Deve Hüyük and other sites, and they are linked with further graves of slightly different form by their grave-goods. The whole group is now dated to the Persian period, except for a few which may go back into the Babylonian period. The Megiddo tombs of this type are unusual in that they had no grave-goods in them: the only finds were tiny pieces of Roman pottery that must be intrusive. The distribution of such tombs over the whole area from Gezer in the west to Persepolis in the east and the Iranian affinities of the grave-goods where they are present strongly suggests that these are burials of Persian garrison troops stationed at Megiddo. Three similar, undated graves on the eastern slopes (T.232, T.854, T.857) could be contemporary. It may be presumed that already in this first phase of Stratum I, from the late sixth century, the fortress on the east side of the mound had been reoccupied. It is possible that it was built only then, as there is nothing to prove a seventh-century date for its construction and a similar fortress is now known to have been built by the Persians in an early stage of Stratum A–B at Tell Jemmeh.

In the later phase of the Persian period the south of the mound was developed as an area of domestic occupation. It is not clear whether buildings elsewhere on the tell were there from the beginning of Persian occupation or only constructed in this second phase. As noted above, not everything that is drawn on the plan of Stratum I is from the Persian period, and because of their proximity to the surface the remains are often incomplete. It is, however, possible to identify two adjacent houses of an 'open-court' plan (compare those of the Assyrian period described on p. 99) in Area A, and a building with three long parallel rooms near the earlier gate may have been barracks for the garrison troops.

The finds from this period are rather undistinguished and include few examples of the fine metalwork and imported goods which are common in contemporary levels elsewhere. The local pottery is typical of the period, showing further influence from Phoenicia. The clay itself of many of the vessels is of a type characteristic of the coastal region, which was dominated by the Phoenicians, rather than the Judaean and Samaritan sites in the hill-country. That Megiddo lay in an area that was little known to the Jews and regarded by them as alien and indeed pagan is suggested by a reference to it in a late post-exilic text: 'On that day the mourning in Jerusalem will be as great as the mourning for Hadad-rimmon in the plain of Megiddo.' (Zechariah 12.11) Hadad-rimmon (or rather, as Assyrian texts show, 'Hadad-ramman') was a form of the storm-god who was worshipped in Damascus already in the ninth century (1 Kings 15:18, 2 Kings 5:18), not, as was once thought, a place-name. The mourning referred to seems to be a fertility ritual in which the summer drought is attributed to the death of the storm-god and lamentations for his demise are thought to bring about the return of the rains in the autumn. The comparison in Zechariah 12:11 suggests that it was a 'great' festival to which people came from far and wide. There is no evidence from the excavations that it was held at Megiddo itself, although some fertility figurines, of traditional type but with some new features, were found in Stratum I.

The little evidence which there is of imported goods is sufficient to show that the occupation at Megiddo lasted throughout the Persian period, but no longer. Three sherds of Attic black-figure lekythoi are reported, dating from between the mid-sixth century and the mid-fifth century, while two Attic lamps from the middle of the fourth century indicate approximately the lower limit of the occupation. A fifth-century Athenian silver didrachma found by Schumacher and four Tyrian coins of the fourth century indicate a similar range (plate 20). Alexander the Great's march through Palestine after the capture of Tyre (322 BC) almost certainly took him past Megiddo, and either this or the troubled times which followed his death would provide a possible occasion for the abandonment of the city and the dispersal of its population.

From the following centuries there are no remains on the tell apart from a succession of coins, dropped perhaps by soldiers or others who climbed the hill for its commanding view, which mark the commercial and political relations of Palestine under Ptolemies, Seleucids, Hasmonaeans, Romans and

Plate 20  Tyrian silver didrachma, dated to the mid-fourth century BC. (*Megiddo I*, figure 124.9)

Arabs. At some time before AD 120 a Jewish village called Kefar 'Otnay (Caparcotnae) came into existence nearby. It is mentioned twice in the Mishnah (Gittin 1:5, 7:7) as a place on the border between Galilee and Samaria, where Rabban Gamaliel II (*c*.AD 100) once pronounced a bill of divorce valid although it had been witnessed by two Samaritans. Its remains probably lie at the base of the deep occupation debris at Lejjun, a kilometre and a half from the tell close by where the road from the south emerges from the Carmel hills. Evidence from milestones shows that early in the reign of Hadrian (AD 117–138) the Legio II Traiana was stationed here, perhaps already occupying the site of the Roman camp a kilometre south-east of Lejjun which was described by Schumacher. This legion's arrival doubled the strength of the Roman force in Palestine, a measure which can be seen as a response to disturbances in the Jewish communities through much of the Roman empire in AD 115–17. After the second Jewish revolt (AD 132–5), and possibly already before it, the Legio VI Ferrata took its place and was stationed at Kefar 'Otnay, as we know both from some inscriptions from Pisidian Antioch which name one of the legionaries and from a broken brick found by Schumacher which was stamped: LEG VI F (figure 22). Eventually the town was renamed Legio, after the occupying force, and from this the Arab town of Lejjun in turn derived its name. Legio became the centre of an administrative district corresponding in extent to the plain formerly known as 'the plain of Megiddo' and an episcopal see, and the extensive Roman remains described by Schumacher, which include a theatre and a palace, provide further evidence of its importance which has yet to be explored thoroughly by archaeologists. About AD 300 it

110

was given the official title of Maximianopolis, after Diocletian's co-ruler Maximian, but the old name, Legio, persisted alongside the new one and in the

Figure 22  Stamped brick fragment of the Sixth Legion found near the Roman theatre (Andrew Brown; based on *Tell el-Mutesellim I*, figure 261)

end outlived it. The remains from the centuries of Arab rule, when Lejjun continued to be a town of note, are also considerable and await investigation. From these periods there are a few isolated structures on the tell: three tombs from the Roman or Byzantine period, and an Arab watchtower, excavated and described by Schumacher, which occupied the favoured position in the east overlooking the plain. With the latter are probably to be associated a cistern a little to the north and a pool in the south of the mound which was later rebuilt as a burial place.

*Further reading*

*Megiddo I* and Schumacher's report provide most of the material relating to these later periods. The latter (vol. I, pp. 173–90) gives the only detailed account of the ruins at Lejjun. On the Persian period generally see the comprehensive work by E. Stern, *Material Culture of the Land of the Bible in the Persian Period, 538–332 BC* (Warminster, 1982), especially pp. 5–8, 240, which deal with Megiddo. I am indebted to Dr P. R. S. Moorey for pointing out to me the parallels from elsewhere to the cist tombs of the Persian period. The identification of Kefar 'Otnay with Legio was first proposed by E. Ritterling, in *Rheinisches Museum* N.F.58 (1903), 633–5 (cf. W. M. Ramsay, *Journal of Roman Studies* 6 (1916), 129–31). For the milestone evidence see B. Isaac and I. Roll, *Zeitschrift für Papyrologie und Epigraphik* 33 (1979), 149–56, and *Latomus* 38 (1979), 54–66. The history of the whole area, with special emphasis on the Roman period, is sketched by the same authors in their *Roman Roads in Judaea I: The Legio-Scythopolis Road*, British Archaeological Reports, International Series, 141 (Oxford, 1982).

Plate 21 Aerial view of the tell from the west: numbers refer to main features visible today – for key see *Appendix: A Visit to the Site* (R. L. W. Cleave: Pictorial Archive Inc, Jerusalem)

# Appendix:

# A Visit to the Site

Megiddo is easily accessible by road from Tel Aviv, Haifa, Nazareth and Tiberias. The express bus-service between Tel Aviv and Tiberias stops at Tzomet Megiddo crossroads, from which it is a walk of about one and a half kilometres to the tell.

Visitors to archaeological sites who have read a book like this one are often disappointed by the scarcity of the remains which they find or can identify. It is of course an inevitable consequence of the process of excavation that many structures, especially of the later periods, are completely removed. This has happened at Megiddo, but an impressive array of well-signposted structures remains to be seen. Some objects from the excavations are also on show in the small museum. The site is well worth a visit and the following notes are designed, with the help of an aerial photograph (plate 21) and references to earlier pages in this book, to enable visitors to place what they can see in its historical context.

The car-park, museum and reception area are situated on the north-east side of the tell and are approached by a side-road off the main road from Haifa.

Ascend by the path to the gate area (1), passing on the right the stepped approach to a water-channel (pp. 81–2) and part of the Solomonic outer gate. Ahead lies the eastern half of the foundations of the Solomonic inner gate, with a few stones of the 'Stratum III' gate visible on top (pp. 80–3, 96). Below and to the right parts of the Canaanite gate of Stratum VIII can be seen (p. 57) and a path leads further to the right to the earlier gate and city wall of Stratum XIII (Middle Bronze I; pp. 38–9).

Turning left past the Solomonic inner gate, the path has on its left walls of the public building of Stratum VIII in Area DD (p. 58) and further along is the area of Yadin's excavation in the Solomonic 'Fortress 6000' (2) (pp. 87–8). The deep, wide cut beyond is Area BB of the American excavations (3), in which can be seen the rectangular Chalcolithic shrine (p. 26), the round stone altar built in Early Bronze II (p. 28) and the three temples of EB IV–MB I (pp. 30–3). On the surface to the south of the cut are some walls of Building 338 and the city wall of the Israelite city (4), which date from the ninth century BC. From this point Schumacher's north–south trench (5) is easily discerned, with

113

walls of the *Nordburg* and *Mittelburg* at the bottom (pp. 43–5). Beyond are houses of the Stratum III city of the Assyrian occupation (6) (pp. 98–9).

Following the path we pass the deep grain storage pit of Stratum III (7) (p. 98), which lies close by the original entrance to the courtyard of Solomon's 'southern palace' (Building 1723) (8) (p. 80) and the abandoned trial trench CC (p. 20), and come to the 'Southern Stables' (9) of the ninth century BC (p. 82). A little to the west is the open shaft (10) giving access to the water supply, of the same date, and it is possible to descend and walk through the well-lit rock-cut tunnel (pp. 92–3). From the exit, outside the city walls, there is a path to return to the gate area. To the west of the shaft is the 'Gallery' approach to the spring (11), from the time of Solomon (pp. 92–3).

The cemetery (12) and the Roman theatre lie to the right (west) of the road on the way back to the Tzomet Megiddo crossroads.

*Further reading*

J. Murphy O'Connor, *The Holy Land: An Archaeological Guide from Earliest Times to 1700* (Oxford, 1980), is an excellent guide to this and all the other main archaeological sites. See also J. M. Miller, *Introducing the Holy Land. A Guidebook for First-Time Visitors* (London, 1983).